CAMBRIDGE LIBRARY COLLECTION

Books of enduring scholarly value

Travel and Exploration

The history of travel writing dates back to the Bible, Caesar, the Vikings and the Crusaders, and its many themes include war, trade, science and recreation. Explorers from Columbus to Cook charted lands not previously visited by Western travellers, and were followed by merchants, missionaries, and colonists, who wrote accounts of their experiences. The development of steam power in the nineteenth century provided opportunities for increasing numbers of 'ordinary' people to travel further, more economically, and more safely, and resulted in great enthusiasm for travel writing among the reading public. Works included in this series range from first-hand descriptions of previously unrecorded places, to literary accounts of the strange habits of foreigners, to examples of the burgeoning numbers of guidebooks produced to satisfy the needs of a new kind of traveller - the tourist.

The North Georgia Gazette and Winter Chronicle

Alone, months of sailing separating them from home, in the polar winter where the sun never rises, the two ships of Captain William Parry's expedition lay encased in ice from November 1819 to March 1820. In order to fully chart the North-West Passage between the Atlantic and the Pacific, it was necessary to overwinter in the Arctic, something that no other British expedition had done before. To boost morale in these uncomfortable circumstances, Captain Edward Sabine (1788–1883), a senior scientist carrying out measurements of natural phenomena, founded and edited a weekly magazine, which ran for twenty-one issues and was made available to the wider world in 1821. Offering jokes, poems, stories and thinly disguised gossip, the members of the expedition contributed to the magazine with enthusiasm (after having first thawed their ink). This little book offers unique insight into what polar exploration in the nineteenth century was actually like.

T0345814

Cambridge University Press has long been a pioneer in the reissuing of out-of-print titles from its own backlist, producing digital reprints of books that are still sought after by scholars and students but could not be reprinted economically using traditional technology. The Cambridge Library Collection extends this activity to a wider range of books which are still of importance to researchers and professionals, either for the source material they contain, or as landmarks in the history of their academic discipline.

Drawing from the world-renowned collections in the Cambridge University Library and other partner libraries, and guided by the advice of experts in each subject area, Cambridge University Press is using state-of-the-art scanning machines in its own Printing House to capture the content of each book selected for inclusion. The files are processed to give a consistently clear, crisp image, and the books finished to the high quality standard for which the Press is recognised around the world. The latest print-on-demand technology ensures that the books will remain available indefinitely, and that orders for single or multiple copies can quickly be supplied.

The Cambridge Library Collection brings back to life books of enduring scholarly value (including out-of-copyright works originally issued by other publishers) across a wide range of disciplines in the humanities and social sciences and in science and technology.

The North Georgia Gazette and Winter Chronicle

EDITED BY EDWARD SABINE

CAMBRIDGE
UNIVERSITY PRESS

CAMBRIDGE UNIVERSITY PRESS

Cambridge, New York, Melbourne, Madrid, Cape Town,
Singapore, São Paolo, Delhi, Mexico City

Published in the United States of America by Cambridge University Press, New York

www.cambridge.org
Information on this title: www.cambridge.org/9781108050111

© in this compilation Cambridge University Press 2012

This edition first published 1821
This digitally printed version 2012

ISBN 978-1-108-05011-1 Paperback

NORTH GEORGIA GAZETTE.

THE

NORTH GEORGIA GAZETTE,

AND

WINTER CHRONICLE.

PERFRETA · HACTENUS · NEGATA ·

LONDON:

JOHN MURRAY, ALBEMARLE-STREET.

———

MDCCCXXI.

LONDON :
PRINTED BY WILLIAM CLOWES,
Northumberland-court.

THE Editor of the following Sheets feels it incumbent on him to state, that at the time they were composed, not the remotest idea was entertained of their fulfilling any other purpose than that of relieving the tedium of an Arctic Winter; and perhaps of afterwards affording amusement to a few private friends at home. On the return of the Expedition, the interest which the Public took in all that had passed during the voyage, induced applications for the perusal of the manuscript, which could only be gratified by its publication. In consenting to this measure, the contributors to the North Georgia Gazette are fully aware, that its principal recommendation to the public notice will be considered to arise from the peculiarities of circumstances and of situation under which it was composed; and they trust that they may be allowed to claim from the general reader the same indulgence, which they would have received, had the perusal of the Chronicle been confined to the partial circle to which they originally intended it should have been limited: with this impression, no alteration has been attempted in the respective papers, in preparing them for the press.

EDWARD SABINE.

LONDON, APRIL 20th, 1821.

PROPOSALS

FOR THE ESTABLISHMENT OF A NEWSPAPER

ON BOARD THE SHIPS EMPLOYED IN THE

DISCOVERY OF A NORTH-WEST PASSAGE.

———————

IT has been suggested that the establishment of a Weekly Newspaper may assist in enlivening the tedious and inactive months of winter. It is in contemplation, therefore, to try the experiment, by circulating the first Number of the " WINTER CHRONICLE" amongst the Officers of the Expedition, on Monday the 1st of November.

As the design of this Paper is solely to promote good-humour and amusement, Captain Sabine, who has undertaken to be the Editor, will consider himself responsible, that no article whatsoever shall be admitted which, to his knowledge, will give a moment's uneasiness to any individual. He reserves to himself, therefore, a discretionary power of omitting any contributions which may appear to him objectionable, either on that or any other account; and, of either briefly assigning his reasons, or otherwise, as he may think proper.

He begs it, however, to be distinctly understood, that he will be wholly dependant on the Gentlemen of the Expedition for the support of the Paper; and, he suggests to those who are well-wishers to the undertaking, that their assistance and exertions will be especially required at its commencement.

Original contributions on any subject will be acceptable. The Sportsman and the Essayist, the Philosopher and the Wit, the Poet and the Plain Matter-of-fact Man, will each find their respective places. It is recommended that an anonymous signature be affixed to each communication, and the hand-writing effectually disguised, to ensure the most rigid impartiality in judging and selecting the articles for insertion. A box will be placed on the Capstan of the Hecla to receive them, the key of which will be kept by the Editor ; and it is requested that communications, designed to appear in the first Number, may be deposited in the box by the Thursday Evening preceding the Publication.

Winter Harbour,
      October 20th, 1819.

CONTENTS.

_____

CONTENTS.

THE
NORTH GEORGIA GAZETTE,

PER·FRETA·HACTENUS·NEGATA·

AND
WINTER CHRONICLE.

N°. I—MONDAY, NOVEMBER 1, 1819.

WE feel great pleasure in being enabled to commence our Editorial Office, by acknowledgments of the lively interest with which the proposals for the establishment of our Paper have been so generally received; of the support with which the demand for the early exertions of our well-wishers has been met; and of the encouragement which we derive from the communications with which we have been already favoured. The proposals having announced a first Number as an experiment, we should feel ourselves wanting in the confidence which the number and respectability of our correspondents so justly inspire, were we to hesitate in declaring our conviction, that the experiment has succeeded; and in venturing, in the name of its supporters, to promise the continuation of the *North Georgia Gazette and Winter Chronicle.*

Having premised thus much, we proceed to lay before our readers the contents of the Editor's box.

———

TO THE
ÉDITOR *of the* WINTER CHRONICLE.

———

Mr. EDITOR—It was with real pleasure I saw in circulation among us, your proposals for a Weekly Newspaper, to be supported by original contributions from the Gentlemen of the Expedition. I am confident that such a paper will, under your censorship, be productive of much amusement, and serve to relieve the *tædium* of our hundred days of darkness *; and, in this view, we cannot but consider you entitled to our best thanks for having undertaken so troublesome an office for the public good.

Having before known more than one *press*

* The sun was ninety-six days below the horizon.

B

of this kind established on board ships, I may take the liberty of warning you not to be discouraged by the slender contributions which the first or second week may be expected to pour into your box. True wit may (for ought you or I know, Mr. Editor,) be as modest as true worth of any other kind, and we must not mistake that for incapacity which may proceed only from diffidence.

The interest which I take in your present plan has, however, enabled me to do more than speculate upon the probable support which your publication will receive at our hands; for you must know, that, soon after I met with your proposals, I took such a liking to them, that I immediately set to work to find out what effect they would have upon our community at large, and I have now much pleasure in assuring you, in the language of our London journals, " that they have produced a great sensation in the public mind."

The very day after your Prospectus appeared, as my reporters inform me, there was a greater demand for ink than has been known during the whole voyage, the green baize of our mess tables has been ever since covered with innumerable pen-parings, to the great detriment, by-the-by, of one of our servants, whose finger has been terribly festered by a prick he received in sweeping them off; and I have it from authority, on which you may rely, that Serjeant Martin* has, within the last week, sharpened no less than nine penknives.

It has been remarked that our tables absolutely groan under the weight of writing desks, which for months past have not seen " the blessed light ;" and it is well known that the holds have been more than once opened of late, for the express, though not

professed, purpose of getting up fresh packages of paper, originally intended for next year's consumption, but which is now destined to grace your file.

" One gentleman," says my correspondent, " more sly than the rest, thought he had eluded our vigilance ; his chest lay in the hatchway to be opened, he took the opportunity, while he thought nobody was looking, to wrap some old clothes round the square package of paper, before he lifted it out. But as he was walking off with them into his cabin, I saw one of the corners of the tin box shining bright through an unfortunate hole in an old flannel waistcoat. When I taxed him with it, he coloured deeply, (strong symptoms, Mr. Editor!) and ran off, declaring most vehemently, that it was only a canister of gingerbread nuts ! ' Nuts, indeed, they were,' adds my facetious friend, ' nuts for the editor !'"

Nor is the information, of which I am in possession, confined simply to this ; for I have pryed more deeply into the business, and have before me secret intelligence of no less than seven literary contributions in embryo, with which the brains of as many youthful compositors have been teeming ever since your Prospectus appeared. I could tell you, if I chose, to which department, among those you have enumerated, each of these belongs ; but as I have no doubt that they will all appear in your pages in their proper time and place, I shall say no more at present about them.

For my own part, Mr. Editor, such is the opinion I entertain of your plan, that I have resolved, unless you lay upon me an absolute prohibition, to make a copy of each paper while it is in circulation. For, I confess, that I anticipate from your pages a fund of rational amusement, not only for the even-

* The serjeant of the Royal Artillery who accompanied Captain Sabine.

ings of this our arctic winter, but for those of many a future one, which we all hope to spend happily in Old England ; and I cannot help looking forward to the time when a paragraph of the *Winter Chronicle*, read aloud around some cheerful fire-side, may draw a tear of pride and pleasure from the eye of an aged parent, an affectionate wife, or a beloved sister.

I remain, Mr. Editor,

Your friend and well-wisher,

PHILO COMUS.

P.S. I forgot to mention to you, that I have some reason to suspect an attempt will occasionally be made to slide into your box communications which are not *quite* original, and therefore not quite corresponding with your plan ; for a gentleman was seen at his desk late the other night, with a volume of the *Spectator* before him, while he was thawing his ink over a lamp. With all due deference to your extensive reading, I think it right to put you on your guard against such attempts; for I have no idea, Mr. Editor, of being obliged to read in the *Winter Chronicle* what our great grandfathers conned over at their breakfast tables more than a century ago.

─────

For the WINTER CHRONICLE.

THE travels of the renowned Baron Munchausen, which I recollect reading when a boy, furnish strong proofs of the very singular effects resulting from extreme cold ; and as it seems probable we may have to encounter a greater severity of weather than even that illustrious personage experienced, I think any idea conducive to the general or individual good of our companions, should not be hoarded in selfish concealment, but liberally given to this little world.

After the frost shall have exhausted all its usual effects of fixing the brandy bottle to the lips, freezing the water in the tea-kettle on the fire, congealing sounds, converting sighs into showers of snow and briny tears into icicles, is it not probable that it may reduce the temperature of the human body so low, as to interfere with the internal economy, compelling the blood to roll through the veins and arteries in the form of peas, dropping one by one into the proper cavities of the heart, and being again discharged from thence like small shot? Now, when matters shall have arrived at such a pitch as this, there is something in the heart, stomach, or bowels, (I think the former,) of many young men called *love*, which though very hot in its nature, must at length acknowledge the frigorific influence. What then will be the result? We know that, even in the comparatively warm climate of Russia, some sorts of liquor are frozen to such a degree, that the whole strength is concentrated, perhaps, into one five-hundredth part of its original space. Now, should this be the case with love, fierce and burning in its present state, to what a deplorable situation must it reduce the unfortunate victim?— if he attempts to breathe, emitting flames like a fabled dragon, while the dissolving blood rushes along in copious streams, and after each respiration as suddenly congeals. But, oh horror ! horror ! should he have accustomed himself to the use of spirits—on the first kindling of the flame, up he goes like a shell, a mine, a rocket ! Think of this, in time, gentle youths, whose sensibility may have betrayed you into love, who " have drank the soft poison of a speaking eye." Root it from your bosoms ere the catastrophe arrives, with persevering fortitude and resolution, and deposit this soft delusive something where it may be at hand for use in a milder clime ; there only can it avail :—then, when the moment arrives which shews you the other terrific symptoms I have mentioned, you will hail me as your friend, your guardian, your benefactor.

FROSTICUS.

Should my conjectures prove correct, would it not be a national benefit to make a turnpike-road from Hudson's Bay to this dreary region? How many married pairs might here revive the almost extinct sparks of regard, and as soon as their bosoms were sufficiently warmed, set off and avoid the dangers of combustion!

For the WINTER CHRONICLE.

ARCTIC MISERIES.

Going out in a winter morning for the purpose of taking a walk, and before you have proceeded ten yards from the ship, getting a cold bath in the cook's steep hole*.

When on a hunting excursion, and being close to a fine deer, after several attempts to fire, discovering that your piece is neither primed nor loaded, while the animal's four legs are employed in carrying away the body.

Setting out with a piece of new bread in your pocket on a shooting party, and when you feel inclined to eat it, having occasion to observe that it is so frozen that your teeth will not penetrate it.

Being called from table by intelligence that a wolf is approaching the vessels, which on closer inspection, proves to be a dog ; on going again below, detecting the cat in running off with your dinner.

Returning on board your ship after an evening visit in a contemplative humour, and being roused from a pleasing reverie by the close embrace of a bear.

Sitting down in anticipation of a comfortable breakfast, and finding that the tea, by mistake, is made of salt water.

OLD COMICAL.

ON THE COMMENCEMENT OF THE WINTER CHRONICLE.

TO enliven the moments, while Winter steals on
With a too tardy pace, be the care of each one ;
Let rancour and malice be banish'd afar,
Unworthy the pen or the heart of a tar !
The fire of true wit may shine vivid and bright,
Untinctured with satire—unprompted by spite :
We are few, and immured in a desolate spot,
Then let envy, resentment, and pride be forgot ;
And while Fate may keep us near one another,
Let each one consider his friend as a brother ;
We shall still find enough to enlarge on, no doubt,
Tho' we have not the charms of a ball or a rout.

* A hole in the ice for steeping salt meat, &c.

The mind philosophic may often impart
Some instruction from nature, some process of art;
Morality too may embellish the page,
And by soft winning precepts attention engage;
The sportsman with pleasure may lead us to view
The toils and the triumphs he oft has gone through;
And each daily occurrence may somewhat afford,
Not unworthy to offer at Dame Reason's board:
And thus each unfolding the gifts of his mind,
While diffusing his knowledge, yet haply may find,
That though what he gives ne'er reduces his store,
He oft by this intercourse adds something more.
Then let me solicit a part of your leisure
To be weekly devoted to giving us pleasure;
And thus I conclude with good wishes most fervent,
And beg to subscribe your obsequious servant,

ALBERT.

_____

For the WINTER CHRONICLE.

TO chase the dull inactive hours away,
Resolved *nem. con.*, that we should have a play;
The play is fix'd on—characters all cast,
Parts learnt, and lo! the first rehearsal past!
Glum cried—" 'Twill do, but to ensure success,
" You'll ask some friend to write you an address."
" Eh?" quoth the Manager—" adzooks, your right,
" Without a *dress* we're in a pretty plight;
" But who shall write it? Marry, there's the rub;
" We have no commerce with that street called Grub."
Strut seem'd perplex'd—look'd thoughtful—took his snuff,
" Egad, I have it—let us send for Puff*!
" Puff is our man—he'll spin us his heroics,
" And melt the audience, if they are not stoics."
" You want a *Puff*," cries Glum—" that's very true,
But, Mr. Puff, I tell you, will not do;
" He'd write, no doubt a mighty pretty story,
" Tell you of England's pride, of England's glory;
" How that her sons advent'rous sallied forth,
" And what's been done in regions thus far north:
" But this, I take it, is too fine by half,
" We want, my friends, something to make us laugh;
" Something to help a lame dog o'er the stile,
" And make our play a tedious hour beguile."

* The part of *Puff*, in *Miss in her Teens*, was to be performed by Mr. Wakeham, who wrote the opening address.

" Still Puff's our man," cried Strut, " I have no doubt
" He'll do the thing, and bring all this about;
" For tho' he dabbles high in epic lore,
" He can descend and make the boxes roar;—
" Ay, Pit and Gallery too—for he is a poet
" Of more than common stamp, and you shall know it."
Thus, Mr. Editor, the affair was settled,
Strut was well pleased, and Glum appeared half nettled;
While we look forward to the eventful night,
To prove Glum wrong—the manager quite right.

Theatre Royal, North Georgia.

The Public are respectfully informed, that the Theatre will open, for
the first time,

ON FRIDAY NEXT, NOVEMBER 5, 1819,

When will be performed Garrick's celebrated Farce of

MISS IN HER TEENS;

OR,

THE MEDLEY of LOVERS.

MEN.

Sir Simon Loveit, Mr. NIAS.   Captain Loveit, Mr. GRIFFITHS.
  Captain Flash, Mr. BUSHNAN.   Fribble, Mr. PARRY.
  Jasper, Mr. HOPPNER.   Puff, Mr. WAKEHAM.

WOMEN.

Miss Biddy, Mr. BEECHEY.   Aunt, Mr. BEVERLEY.
           Tag, Mr. HOOPER.

SONGS, by Messrs. SKENE, PALMER, and BUSHNAN, will be introduced
between the Acts.

Previous to the Performance,

AN APPROPRIATE ADDRESS,

Written expressly for the Occasion,

Will be spoken by Mr. WAKEHAM.

Doors will open at Half-past Six, and the Curtain will rise precisely at Seven.

TO CORRESPONDENTS.

ALBERT'S Enigma in our next.

AMICUS'S " Prologue to *Miss in her Teens*, to be spoken after the opening Address," has been received. The Editor takes the liberty of suggesting, that the Manager of the Theatre is the person to whom it should have been sent. It is not yet too late to be so sent; and when spoken, it would appear in due course in our Theatrical Report.

We are requested to state, that a humorous Epilogue to *Miss in her Teens* would add considerably to the amusements of Friday evening.

NAUTICUS'S communication, entitled " A Problem," has been received. We take this opportunity to remark, that we consider that it falls within the plan of our Paper, to admit questions which may exercise the ingenuity of our Readers, and furnish occupation in their solution; but it is necessary, in order to render such questions worthy the occasion, that they should possess a certain degree of originality, and require more than a *very ordinary* knowledge to resolve them. If our friend Nauticus will refer to any of the Elementary Treatises on Arithmetic or Algebra, he will find under the Rules of Position, or of Simple Equations, many very similar examples to his, proposed for the student's instruction, and the mode of their resolution explained.

THE
NORTH GEORGIA GAZETTE,

AND
WINTER CHRONICLE.

Nº. II—MONDAY, NOVEMBER 8, 1819.

SINCE our first Number has been in circulation, we have received various communications of encouragement, and assurances of support, confirming the persuasion which we ventured to avow in our last Number, that the Winter Chronicle is no longer an experiment. As in the days of unconquered Rome, it was deemed no less than a capital offence to entertain doubts of the safety of the commonwealth; so we certainly will not set the example of bad citizenship, by permitting a suspicion to take possession of our minds, that the united talents and exertions of our little community will prove inadequate to support a design which is deemed conducive to the public good.

From the above-mentioned communications we have selected the one which we present to our readers, from a correspondent who signs himself " A plain Matter-of-Fact Man," because it coincides with our own sentiments on the subject.

MR. EDITOR—I hope you will not think me behind-hand in assuring you of the pleasure I received on reading your proposals circulated amongst us—a pleasure not less sincere than that of those who have been before me in expressing it. I felt also the propriety of your appeal to your well-wishers for their timely support, and counting myself in that number, I was very desirous to have complied with your request; but, Mr. Editor, I will freely confess, that after puzzling my head a long time to no purpose, I was forced to give the matter up, in utter despair of finding a subject upon which " A plain Matter-of-Fact Man," as I profess myself to be, could address you with any prospect of entertainment to your readers. Yet, as day passed after day, I felt less and less satisfied to rest without making an attempt, at least, to contribute my portion to the general fund.

The object of your Paper being our amusement, I consider it alike the interest and business of every individual who is pleased with such an establishment amongst us, to do something towards its support; for if we do not furnish you with communications, Mr. Editor, nothing is more plain than that you cannot furnish us with papers: and, if during the winter, a Monday shall arise without a *Winter Chronicle* to grace our breakfast-tables, we shall, indeed, by our backwardness have deprived ourselves (in words so justly and feelingly used by your correspondent Philo-Comus, and which I repeat to impress them more strongly on your readers) of " A source of rational amusement not only for the evenings of this our Arctic Winter, but of many a future one, when a paragraph of the *Winter Chronicle*, read aloud around some cheerful fireside, may draw a tear of pride and pleasure from the eye of an aged parent, an affectionate wife, or a beloved sister."

You will readily conceive, then, Mr. Editor, that I was not a little cheered at the satisfaction which you expressed in your first Number, and at the confident manner in which you announced your persuasion of further and sufficient aid. But, do not suppose that your correspondents hitherto have borne any proportion, in point of number, to that of your well-wishers, or of those who will eventually assist in filling your columns. I have reason to know, that I was not singular in the embarrassment which deprived me of the gratification of seeing my signature in the list of your earliest contributors : and, that there are not a few persons who are only waiting to form their

judgment on the sort of communication which will be acceptable, and who will fall into your ranks, one by one.

I would, therefore, add my voice to that of your more experienced correspondent, Philo-Comus, that you be not discouraged by the slender contributions of the first few weeks.

I would also remind those who are yet silent from the cause which has been just assigned, that *now* is the time when support is most needed; when, if every person will put his shoulder to the wheel in earnest, (and each individual may command his own exertions,) there can be no doubt that your Paper will go on with spirit.

Permit me to subscribe myself,

your occasional Correspondent,

A plain Matter-of-Fact Man.

THEATRICAL REPORT.

The theatre opened on Friday evening with the farce of " Miss in her Teens," preceded by an address, written and spoken by Mr. Wakeham.

We have been favoured with a copy of this production, with which we shall present our readers in one of our subsequent columns. We have only to express our persuasion that there can be but one opinion of its merit, and shall only add, that we think the *Actor* scarcely did justice to the *Author*; probably from the diffidence natural to a man in reciting his own verses.

Two appropriate songs were introduced between the acts, by Messrs. Skene and Palmer, and were received with much applause.

Having been obligingly furnished with copies of them, we shall offer no apology to our readers for inserting them for their perusal. We understand that these are also from the pen of Mr. Wakeham; nor have we yet stated, if we are rightly informed, the extent of our obligation to his Muse, since we derived much amusement from an epilogue said to be written by him for the occasion, at a few hours' notice, and spoken with great spirit by Mrs. Tag and Jasper, in character: we regret that our limits do not allow us to give this production a place in our pages.

Persons who are not familiar with the expedients which are resorted to, to produce effect with very deficient means, would have been astonished at the manner in which this entertainment was got up, under circumstances the most disadvantageous that can be conceived; for, we know that not an article of scenery, decorations, or dresses, was embarked in either ship for this purpose, and yet we venture to assert, that few provincial theatres in England would have excelled ours in either of these respects.

The scenery was painted under the direction of Lieutenant Beechey, who has also obligingly undertaken the management of the theatre.

The characters were supported throughout with great spirit and propriety, and we consider that our thanks are especially due to the gentlemen who took the female parts, which were performed with no inconsiderable share of animation, and feminine delicacy.

At the conclusion of the epilogue, the street-scene rising, discovered the whole of the Dramatis Personæ, who struck up " God save the King," in which they were joined by many of the audience with great enthusiasm, and the curtain fell amid loud and repeated applause.

We congratulate the performers, as well as the rest of our community, upon this successful commencement of our theatrical entertainments. Amusement was the sole object for which they were undertaken—that object has thus far been completely accomplished, and we sincerely trust that nothing will occur to prevent their regular continuance.

We are aware that to effect this, there are many difficulties to overcome. We understand that one of the most serious of these, and which proves how little expectation was formed of our having leisure or inclination to attempt a play during the voyage, is the very small collection of dramatic works which the manager has been able to muster in both ships; so that it becomes a matter not of choice, but of necessity, to act those only which happen to be on board.

A considerable proportion of these must of course, be unfit for the limited means which our theatre possesses; but we feel persuaded that nothing will be left undone to give them all the effect which these means afford.

We cannot conclude our report without indulging for a moment one pleasing consideration, which the occasion naturally suggests.

What delight would not our friends in England experience, could they be informed of our present situation, and of the means we are thus employing to render it, not merely tolerable, but cheerful and happy! If any incitement were wanting to make each of us persevere in contributing his share towards the general amusement, this consideration would amply furnish it: nor should we fail to remark, that cheerfulness, which is always amiable as a *private* virtue, becomes in *our* case, almost a *public* duty; and, that he who uses his best endeavours to encourage it, takes at once the most effectual method to promote his own comfort, and to benefit the public service.

c

ADDRESS

ON THE OPENING OF THE THEATRE ROYAL, NORTH GEORGIA,

WRITTEN AND SPOKEN BY MR. WAKEHAM.

REPOS'D from war—triumphant in the field
Where rescu'd Europe's destiny was seal'd;
No foe to combat on the rolling wave,
No injur'd monarch that her sword might save,
'Twas still our much lov'd country's glorious claim
To stand pre-eminent, unmatch'd in fame,
And in the paths of Science yet to find
The liberal plan to benefit mankind.
Far in the North an unknown region lay,
Where growing ice congeal'd the liquid way.
Yet here it seem'd Columbia's bending shore,
Stretch'd westward, heard Pacific Ocean's roar.
  Full oft in earlier days, had Britons tried
To force a passage through the arrested tide,
But tried in vain, tho' with intrepid skill
Persisting long, in spite of ev'ry ill.
By happier fortune led, 'twas ours to prove
Thus far, uncheck'd by land, the waters rove,
And ice-encumber'd here to win our way
'Mid the long sunshine of an arctic day.
  But now for coming storms and frigid air
Approaching Winter bids us well prepare,
The Sun retiring * scarce illumes the sky,
Swift driving snows in circling eddies fly,
And soon no gladd'ning ray shall gild our noon,
But from the radiant stars, or changing moon.
While thus inactive we are doom'd to stay,
To cheer the ling'ring hours—behold a play.
And tho' we boast not power by scenic art
To warm the passions, or affect the heart;
Yet here secure we tread—no critic's eye
Is bent, with eager gaze, each fault to spy;
Amusement all our aim, if that succeed,
Our wish is gain'd—nor ask we other meed.

---

* The day preceding that on which this Address was spoken was the last that we had seen the sun
  above the horizon for an interval of ninety-six days.

But, when emerging from stern Winter's tomb,
Reviving Spring shall chase the dreary gloom,
And genial warmth, expanding o'er the plain,
Pour melting snows in torrents to the main,
When rustling winds, with all resistless sweep,
Unlock the fetter'd surface of the deep—
Then with new ardour will we onward hie
To seek a passage 'neath this Polar sky;
Firm in our Leaders' care, who still have shewn
The great resolve, the daring deed their own.
Nor—if that Power, whose providential sway
The burning suns and meaner orbs obey,
Approving smile—will we the task give o'er
Till southern surges round our vessels roar;
Then with glad sails we'll plough the foaming seas,
Delighted, list'ning to the swelling breeze
That swift impels us to Britannia's shore,
To love, to friendship, and our homes once more.

For the WINTER CHRONICLE.

ENIGMA.

I owe my birth to every clime
Found in the spacious rolls of time.
Proud cities have I overthrown,
Yet am subservient to a clown;
Nor, if he wishes, can refuse
To dress his food, or clean his shoes.
Oft when some pedlar in the street
Has tried too long the practis'd cheat,
To me the rogue they quickly draw,
To punish without form of law.
    In ladies' rooms each morn I'm found,
Preparing for the toilet's round;
I wanton o'er the fragrant breast,
The pouting lips by me are press'd;
Nor does the veriest prude disdain
To use me thus, or e'er complain;
Yet oft, when visits they would make,
If I the fair ones overtake,
They quickly fly me in despair,
And seek a coach, a house, a chair.
The warrior, ere he meets a foe,
Woos me assistance to bestow.

Oft have I kept him from the fight,
Oft check'd at once his hasty flight,
And closed his eyes in endless night.
Britannia owes to me her pow'r,
I keep the Gaul from coming o'er,
And oft have borne her gallant fleet,
To where the foemen they might meet.
My absence has been known to foil
Her sailors' skill and utmost toil;
But when I came their toil was o'er,
And vict'ry theirs, as oft before.
Among the clouds I'm known to dwell,
And frequent from that height I've fell;
Yet sometimes in the ambient air
I float, in form extremely fair;
At others, not the strongest race
Of men could lift me from my place.
I'm near you now, and ev'ry day,
Can you not yet my name display?
Full sure I am, when next you dine,
You'll swallow me before your wine.

ALBERT.

TO CORRESPONDENTS.

One of our Correspondents requests to be informed, whether the lame dog which appeared on the Stage *, when the Address was spoken, be *the lame dog* alluded to by Q in the lines inserted in our last Number.

At the suggestion of another Correspondent, the Editor takes the opportunity of stating, for general information, that the contents of his box will be subject to his inspection alone, and that should the handwriting create any suspicion of the author, it will be confined to himself.

Unacknowledged communications stand over for insertion.

The Songs by Messrs. SKENE and PALMER in our next.

* A dog that had been lamed some time before, and happened to come limping on the Stage immediately after Mr. Wakeham.

THE
NORTH GEORGIA GAZETTE,

PER · FRETA · HACTENUS · NEGATA.

AND
WINTER CHRONICLE.

N°. III—MONDAY, NOVEMBER 15, 1819.

SINCE the publication of Frosticus's letter in our first Number, we have received various communications on the subject which he has treated in so experienced and feeling a manner. Several of our correspondents (and especially so far as we can judge by their style, the *younger* ones,) seem to have become already sensible of the sensations which are there so ably described, although the thermometer has not yet fallen below —35°. The earlier symptoms seem, indeed, to be much the same in all cases, and are expressed with a fluency which persuades us that the writers have them continually at their fingers' ends.

We feel, therefore, that we may be conferring a benefit on the public by inserting, for the perusal of our youthful correspondents in general, the following letter, in which a remedy (vainly sought for in Frosticus's communication, on which account heavy and grievous are the complaints) is proposed for one of the symptoms of this disease, which, without some effort being made to eradicate it, bids fair to become epidemic amongst us : as the author signs himself *Philosophicus*, and writes very unintelligibly about " marrowy succulency, aculeate points," &c., at least to those " whose propensities" have not led them with him to the study of " Phar-ma-co lo-gi-cal works," we conclude that he considers himself well qualified to offer advice in such desperate cases.

Mr. Editor—Having recovered a little from the alarm excited by Frosticus's interesting and scientific letter, I began to ruminate upon the other wonderful phenomena, which the intensity of the cold might produce upon our system. An evil shortly occurred to me, which, although of minor importance in itself, would be productive (if not immediately warded off,) of the dire catastrophe so ably described in the communication alluded to.

As no doubt you are impatient to learn the fruits of my meditations, I shall, without further preamble, proceed to lay them before you.

Having gathered from the medical writers I have perused, (which, by-the-by have been very numerous, as I have a propensity for Pharmacological works,) that hair, like the horn of a bull, goat, or ram, is filled with a marrowy succulency ; and, as a very trifling degree of cold more than what we have experienced, will cause congelation in these exposed parts, the heads and bodies of our little community will be covered with innumerable aculeate points, which, if brought in contact with their own or other people's flesh, will make so many orifices, through which the external air will find an easy access to the inmost recesses of the veins, and immediately produce that extraordinary globosity of the blood, which is so philosophically and prophetically treated by Frosticus.

Now, Mr. Editor, I have no doubt you will concur with me in seeing the necessity (as one mode of guarding against this alarming phenomenon,) of striking at the root of every evil that may produce it ; for which purpose, I propose that every individual cranium, whiskers, &c., be submitted to the tonsorial operator, and that all the instruments which can be mustered, be instantly put in order for the purpose, before the cold renders this step impracticable.

As I am fully aware of the interest you take in the public weal, I trust you will consider my anxiety to avert the impending danger, a sufficient apology for trespassing so long upon your valuable time.

I remain, &c.

Philosophicus.

We hope our correspondents may derive some relief from this learned communication; but as the proposed operation is rather an uncomfortable one, and if not attended by the effects which the writer anticipates, may be a dangerous one in this bleak climate, we take the liberty of suggesting that Philosophicus should first try the experiment upon himself, especially as shaving the head is well known to be efficacious in more cases than one! If after he has submitted his head to the " tonsorial operator," he will favour us with a further communication, and it shall appear that he has himself materially benefited, we are confident that even the most desperate cases will find relief in following his example.

SPEECH

OF

COUNSELLOR PUZZLEWELL,

In the Court of Common Sense, in Arctic Land, before Chief Justice Opinion *and a Special Jury,*

In the Cause Editor *v.* Non Contributors.

" My Lords, and Gentlemen of the Jury,

" After the very able and perspicuous address of my learned friend, Philo-Comus, I should have submitted the cause of my client to your candid and impartial judgment without a remark, had not Mr. Serjeant, ' Plain Matter-of-Fact Man,' besides following my learned brother through almost every point of his statement, charged my clients with neglecting their ' interest and business;' because, forsooth, they were unable or unwilling to ' do something,' just at the time he thinks they ought to do it. Now, my Lord and Gentlemen, as the learned Serjeant has set out with declaring himself equally guilty for a considerable time, and there being no law which fixes a determinate period for the production of ' these somethings,' I conceive the delay will appear to be caused by the tardy operation of nature, which we have frequently seen spreading the useless weed in rank luxuriance, while the delicious fruit and beauteous flower slowly attain perfection.

" Having stated this much in vindication of my clients, I shall await your verdict, in full confidence that it will establish their character as innocent of any transgression against the laws of honour, propriety, and good sense."

After a verdict for the defendants had been pronounced, and received with loud acclamations, the Counsellor informed the Court, that he had been instructed to express the intention of his clients, not to be " behind-hand" in affording the Editor that support to which his strenuous and liberal exertions for the public amusement so justly entitle him.

―――

MR. EDITOR.—The anticipation so pleasingly expressed in your first Number, by your able Correspondent, Philo-Comus, and repeated in the second by the " Plain Matter-of-Fact Man," of a source of rational amusement, &c. &c. &c., had taken such full possession of my mind, that after having idly tortured my invention for something to assist in filling your columns, slumber supplied what my waking thoughts were incapable of producing. I fancied myself vested with the power of removing, at a wish, from place to place, and being troubled with a considerable share of curiosity, as well as a slender portion of taste for science, I was immediately, on reaching England, (of course my first wish), set down in the midst of an assemblage of beauty, fashion, and talent, at Mrs. ――'s in ―― street. As I was unknown I had an opportuuity of contemplating, at leisure, the objects by which I was surrounded; the blaze of loveliness before me occupied my eyes, and my attention for some time; at length I turned to notice the collection of pictures, china vases, &c., ranged around, and pursued them in succession, until the mistress of the mansion attracted my views. A young lady, the image of her mamma, was engaged in conversation with a naval officer; feeling some little anxiety on account of an absent friend, I drew near enough to overhear them, though they spoke low. " And which did you seriously think the safest ship?" were the first words that met my ear; when he named the H――; her eyes sparkled with unusual vivacity, and a blush diffused itself over her lovely cheek; a sigh, no less sudden, succeeded. A valued friend in one perhaps, thought I, a dearer lover in the other. Wanton Cupid, what tricks are you playing with us? The sound had scarcely passed my lips before the scene was changed, and I beheld a young and charming widow, reclining on a sofa, her eyes suffused with tears. She knew me, and passionately cried, " Where is my ――? (secrets must not be told, Mr. Editor), is he returned to bless these fond expecting arms? For pity's sake, keep me no longer in suspense—does he live?" " He does," I tried to say; but a wish rising in my bosom to be acquainted with more secrets, I was hurried away, and in a moment found myself at a fashionable party in —— square. No sooner was my name mentioned, than a crowd of the sweetest creatures I ever beheld surrounded me; in short, they were women, young and beautiful; a deluge of inquiries poured upon me; " How is Mr. ——?" "How does my friend ——?" "I hope Mr. —— is well!" "All well," said I, overcome with such a torrent of prattle, and a smile repaid my intelligence, which equally defied the painter's and the poet's art.

> " 'Twas then I saw
> The soft language of the soul
> Beam from the never silent eye."

A young lady now tripped softly up to inquire after Mr. —— : her air was pensive, and in gentle embarrassment; she lisped something very like " dear," or some such word; then recovering herself, carelessly inquired, " Is he grown!" " I think him rather taller, still sprightly, and charming as ever." She pressed my hand, and thanked me. A swelling sigh escaped.— " Could you give him this ?" She offered it, and then timidly withdrew her hand ! 'Twas a miniature. My own heart had been irretrievably lost in another moment, had I not called reason to my aid, and wished myself away, though I could not determine whither. During this interval of indecision with every varying thought, I flew up and down the street, till unluckily a drowsy watchman crossing my path, was instantly, with lantern and rattle, stretched at full length in the gutter. As I stopped to assist him, his brethren came up and seized me. Burning with indignation at their rude treatment, the desire of revenge fixed me to the spot; and, after cuffing some time,

as I nimbly withdrew my head from the blow of a descending cudgel, it came so furiously in contact with the side of my bed-place, that I was at once re-called to wakefulness and stupidity.

Believe me, Mr. Editor,
your sincere well-wisher,
Philo-Somnus.

THEATRICAL.

WE are requested to insert the following notice from the managers of the theatre : we desire to add that the Editor's box is at all times at the service of the manager and his correspondents, as the medium of their communications.

The manager having no access to " Simon Dogrellicus," except through the public papers, makes an apology for not having acknowledged his communication before. He begs leave to thank him for his song, which being humorous, and likely to afford amusement, will be sung between the acts of the next play. The manager takes the opportunity of informing Simon Dogrellicus, and other Grub-street authors, Philo-Comus, Albert, Q, &c., and the public in general, that plays, prologues, epilogues, songs, ludicrous recitations, &c., will greatly contribute to the general amusement. The theatrical library at present consists of six or seven pieces only, and some of these but badly adapted to our stage. It is, therefore, evident that the house must shut up before the season is over, for few persons, notwithstanding the characters be ever so well supported, will sit out the 199th representation of any one performance : and the manager foresees a lack of applause ; a dry significant sneer at an old joke, for which the audience had been lying in wait for a quarter of an hour, discontented countenances, empty boxes, and finally the fall of the green curtain, to rise no more, unless some one start forth amongst the crowd, invoke the muse, and bid our curtain rise again.   The manager has dwelt thus long on the subject, under a conviction that there is no want of ability, would the gentlemen exert themselves.

Theatre Royal, North Georgia.

POETRY.

WHEN Denmark's Prince appears upon the stage,
(At least we learn so from great Shakspeare's page,)
He steals with slow and solemn majesty,
And thus exclaims—" to be or not to be ?"
But when the Baker*, poor lame dog, appear'd
Upon North Georgia's boards, no voice was heard
From him ; he innocently look'd around,
And scarcely put his fourth foot to the ground ;
The audience smiled—the address was not suspended,
And here, I surely thought, th' affair had ended,
Until your Paper's second number came,
Stating, a Correspondent mark'd how lame
The dog appear'd ; and straight desires to be
Inform'd—" If this dog was, or was *not*, he
That Glum foresaw would come with limping vile,
And need a friend to help him o'er the stile."
I like your Papers—therefore do I read 'em ;
I like your Correspondents—'cause you need 'em.
But give me leave, friend Editor, a word,
The man that asks a question so absurd,
Proves that he has a monstrous lack of brains ;
Yet, not to give offence, I took the pains
To search out Glum, and in a friendly way
Ask him what I in answer now could say.
" Say," replied Glum, " I do not think it fit
" To answer one who shews so little wit."
" In truth, in some respects," I said, " you're right,
" But still you must acknowledge, on that night

---

* The dog having belonged to a baker at Deptford, was so called by the men.

" None of the lameness you so justly fear'd,
" Throughout the play or rather song appear'd."
" Why, to be plain, I scarcely could espy
" A fault, tho' search'd for with a critic's eye;
" Humph—so he thinks to puzzle me, the rogue,
" But I 'll have at him in the epilogue.
" Tell him the Manager, as well as me,
" Saw how much mischief there would surely be,
" Unless great care was ta'en to keep away
" The intruder which I spoke of t' other day;
" Placed Mr. Prompter *, whom he thought a host,
" To guard the door, nor e'er desert his post.
" True to his post, the prompter did a wonder,
" He made the Play pass off without a blunder.
" But when for the Epilogue the curtain rose,
" Wearied with watching, or some other cause,
" He left his post, when, shocking to relate !
" The limper came and stopp'd the lady's prate,
" Which so confused her, off she would have gone,
" Had not the gallantry of every one
" Been put in force, to spare her maiden blushes,
" And drive the dog to beat about the bushes.
'• Thus I shall prove my forethought was not wrong,
" And now good morning—I have staid too long."
In words like these did Glum himself express;
They 're little to the purpose, I confess;
But when your Correspondents send a query,
They must not blame the answer tho' it weary,
And as you think 'twill tire 'em or divert 'em,
You either may omit or else insert 'em.

                                          Q.

* The prompter whose absence from his post during the Epilogue is thus commented upon, was suspected of being the author of the query to which these lines are the reply.

TO CORRESPONDENTS.

We are obliged to postpone the Songs promised in our last.

TIMOTHY SEE-THROUGH-IT has not hit the solution of ALBERT's Enigma.

LAZARUS LACKBRAIN's letter has reached its destination.

THE
NORTH GEORGIA GAZETTE,

PER · FRETA · HACTENUS · NEGATA ·

AND
WINTER CHRONICLE.

Nº. IV—MONDAY, NOVEMBER 22, 1819.

WE owe an apology to Peter Trial, for having delayed the insertion of his letter, until so long a time after the performance to which he alludes. The fact, however, was, that so much of our Second Number had been occupied by the affairs of the theatre, that we had barely room in our last to insert the manager's circular address; and we found ourselves obliged, in justice to our correspondents on other subjects, to postpone the letter which we now submit to our readers, as well as the songs which were sung by Messrs. Skene and Palmer, and which will be found in the present number.

To the EDITOR of the Winter Chronicle.

SIR—I cannot help expressing the infinite delight I felt in witnessing the entertaining performance of Friday evening, which few would hesitate to pronounce as superior to every thing of the kind which has preceded it in this country, and which will never be surpassed by future strollers towards this mild and genial climate.

The North Georgia Theatre, though reared in much less time, and in a greater hurry than Covent Garden or Drury Lane, possesses an advantage over those magnificent structures, which, even their internal decorations and dazzling charms * cannot equal; for, in spite of all their endeavours to procure a free ventilation and a cool atmosphere, they have never yet succeeded like our able architect, Mr. Frost, in this very essential and particular point.

Before I conclude, let me recommend to those performers who have any distance to

* The gas-lights we presume. ED.

return home after the doors are shut, and who may have taken as much refreshment as the house affords, that they be on their guard against the prowling wolf, and the more ferocious bear, and above all the iron hand of Winter; or, when we would speak of them again, they may have become fitter subjects for epitaphs, than to furnish us with the more pleasurable employment of recording their meritorious exploits.

I remain, &c. &c.,

PETER TRIAL.

We would willingly submit to the consideration of our correspondents, both philosophical and otherwise, whether there be any connexion in the way of cause and effect, between the increased severity of the cold in the last week, and the empty state of the Editor's box. We are aware that much may be said very learnedly and hypothetically, from whence the probability of such a connexion may be inferred ; though perhaps on this as on many other points, the less said the stronger may be the inference. Having hinted thus much, we willingly leave the subject to them, in full confidence that it is in their power to cause it by Thursday next to be no longer a question. We wish also with the permission and by the means of our friend *Trim*, to remind the counsellor Puzzle-

well that an engagement made in open court, is so far binding on the party making it, that its due performance may be claimed, and the claim enforced by the authority of the court, in whose presence it was made. Now, as the learned counsellor was instructed by his clients " The Non-Contributors," to express in open court their intention of being no longer " behind-hand" in affording " that support to the Editor," &c. &c.; and, as " that support," &c. &c., has not yet been afforded, we have thought, that if Mr. Serjeant Plain Matter-of-Fact-Man can be prevailed on to be again our advocate, we would employ him to move in the court of Common Sense, that counsellor Puzzlewell be required to shew cause why the fulfilment of the instructions so expressed as above, has been, and still is, delayed.

————

A very ingenious answer to Albert's enigma having been circulated in manuscript during the past week, it remains with us to publish the author's solution as we originally received it.

> In ev'ry clime, remote or near,
> Where'er the eye of man can peer,
> Of general use to human kind
> Prolific *water* you will find.

———————

𝕿𝖍𝖊𝖆𝖙𝖗𝖊 𝕽𝖔𝖞𝖆𝖑, 𝕹𝖔𝖗𝖙𝖍 𝕲𝖊𝖔𝖗𝖌𝖎𝖆.

———

On WEDNESDAY NEXT, the 24th instant,
Will be performed Foote's much admired Comedy of

THE LIAR.

With the usual accompaniment of SONGS between the Acts.
Doors will open at Half past Six, and the Performance will begin at Seven precisely.

———

The Manager has received F. R. S.'s Prologue, and will submit it for consideration at the first meeting of the Commitiee.

SONGS

WRITTEN FOR THE NORTH GEORGIA THEATRE,

BY MR. WAKEHAM,

AND SUNG AT THE PERFORMANCE ON FRIDAY THE 5TH OF NOVEMBER.

SONG, MR. SKENE.

TUNE, *Jessy of Dumblaine.*

OH! what can compare with the beams of the morn,
When the bright sparkling dew-drops bespangle the thorn,
When Aurora's young blushes tint deeper the sky,
'Ere the Sun's flaming orb is yet mounted on high?
'Tis the soft smile of beauty, that beams from the eyes
Of thy daughters, fair Albion! the land that we prize.

When distant, far distant, from all that's held dear,
From the happy fire-side, and the friend that's sincere;
What nerves for the battle the arm of the brave,
Or bid's us encounter the storm-beaten wave?
'Tis the soft smile of beauty, that beams from the eyes
Of thy daughters, fair Albion! the land that we prize.

Tho' thy sons in the field are undaunted in war,
And the fame of thy chieftains resound from afar;
Tho' Nature each charm in thine island combines,
One ray of thy glory all others outshines.
'Tis the soft smile of beauty, that beams from the eyes
Of thy daughters, fair Albion! the land that we prize.

What leads us to traverse these regions unknown,
And explore each recess of this dark frozen zone?
Tho' with thirst of renown every bosom may burn,
What reward do we hope when again we return?
'Tis the soft smile of Beauty, that beams from the eyes
Of thy daughters, fair Albion! the land that we prize.

SONG, MR. PALMER.

Tune, *Sprig of Shillelah.*

SAY, who but has heard that a true British tar
Is kind to his lass, and regards not a scar,
With a heart firm in danger, and constant in love ?
If assail'd by the tempest, or toss'd on the wave,
Each nerve is exerted his vessel to save.
He repairs to the helm to direct her aright,
Or stands at his quarters, expecting the fight,
With a heart firm in danger, and constant in love.

When duty is o'er 'mongst his messmates below,
His mirth and good humour unceasingly flow,
From a heart firm in danger, and constant in love,
He pledges his girl in full bumpers of grog,
Sings his song, for good fellowship ever a-gog,
Enjoys ev'ry hour, as it passes him by,
Unwilling the moments more swiftly should fly,
With a heart firm in danger, and constant in love.

When call'd by his country, he lingers no more,
But leaving the joys of his dear native shore,
With a heart firm in danger, and constant in love.
Embarks to explore Hyperborean coasts
Surrounded by ice, and enfetter'd by frosts,
Regardless of Winter's perpetual reign,
And prepared to encounter the boisterous main,
With a heart firm in danger, and constant in love.

No toil can subdue him, no horrors appal,
A true British tar meets whate'er may befal,
With a heart firm in danger, and constant in love.
Again he shall visit the land of his birth,
Press his girl to his heart, and indulging his mirth,
His travels recounted—his perils told o'er,
Await the high call of his country once more,
With a heart firm in danger, and constant in love.

And well shall Old England remember her son,
Who has added new glories to those she has won,
With a heart firm in danger, and constant in love;
Whose keel ever daring, disparts the proud sea,
That had ne'er borne a ship since the world 'gan to be;
And guided by Providence still shall press on,
Till he rounds the bleak Cape * that has yet stopped each one,
With a heart firm in danger, and constant in love.

Let Britons on shore, then, the bright flowing bowl
Fill high to the Sailor undaunted in soul,
With a heart firm in danger, and constant in love;
And may he, when return'd from the toils of the wave,
Find that Honour and Love still await on the brave,
Who dares for his country, his friends, and his home,
By Freedom inspired, o'er the wide ocean roam,
With a heart firm in danger, and constant in love.

* Icy Cape.

———————

This song was received with every demonstration of interest by the audience, and rapturously encored.

THE
NORTH GEORGIA GAZETTE,

AND
WINTER CHRONICLE.

N°. V—MONDAY, NOVEMBER 29, 1819.

TO THE

EDITOR *of the* WINTER CHRONICLE.

SIR,

AS I was indulging the other evening in profound cogitation, whilst enjoying my segar by the fire-side, the following lines, which I do not exactly remember where first to have seen, struck across my mind as the flitting subject of the moment:

" The Indian leaf doth briefly burn,
" So doth man's strength to weakness turn ;
" The fire of youth extinguished quite,
" Comes age, like embers dry and white :
 " Think of this as you take tobacco."

Seeing a vast deal of truth in the above quotation, and an excellent picture of the mutability of our nature, I trust, Mr. Editor, to be excused in requesting you to give it publicity ; though I recollect something about not inserting things which are borrowed. I only request, then, to be informed, ere it be rejected, in what book these lines are to be found, and from whom they are copied. Or, if you should think fit, in the multiplicity of your concerns, to submit it to your correspondents, and leave it to some one or other of them, in their general acquaintance with every topic minute, learned, scientific or otherwise, to detect the copyist, and make an exposé of him in the following week's Gazette,

 You would oblige,

  Mr. Editor, *&c. &c.*

   PETER FUME.

We have inserted Peter Fume's letter, in the hope that some of our correspondents may know the original author of the lines he has quoted; probably Peter Fume's acquaintance with them is derived from the same source as our own, namely, from Rob Roy, where they are very aptly introduced, Vol. I. Page 206.

LAW REPORT.

COURT OF COMMON SENSE,

In the Cause of EDITOR *v.* NON-CONTRIBU-
TORS.

HIS lordship being seated, Counsellor Puzzlewell rose, and addressed the Court as follows:

MY LORD—I shall not occupy your lordship's time by following my learned brother, the counsel for the plaintiff, through the matter-of-fact reasoning, wherein he considers himself to have proved that, by the custom of this court, it is incumbent on my clients, "The Non-Contributors," to afford that support, &c. &c., the delay of which is the subject now before your lordship; nor shall I question the right which he has claimed to the fulfilment of the promise which I was instructed to make, and did make, in their name. No, my lord, however ready and able I may feel myself to controvert these points, and I doubt not to your lordship's satisfaction, yet as my clients have thought fit rather to concede them, I shall content myself with moving your lordship and the court, that certain affidavits be read, with which I am furnished by my clients, and which I have no doubt will be accounted by your lordship most satisfactory reasons for the delay; and will be deemed sufficient to entitle them to such further indulgence as your lordship shall be pleased to grant, and for which I am instructed to solicit.

The affidavits were then read as follows:

The *Affidavit of* David Drowsy.

This deponent maketh oath and saith, that want of leisure hath hitherto prevented his offering that assistance to the Editor, which his good wishes for the support of the said paper would otherwise have prompted him to afford; that what with the time necessarily occupied in three regular meals, and two little ones per day, a two hours' nap after dinner, and another after coffee, with an occasional doze in the forenoon, together with the duties of his profession in these times of constant activity, he most positively deposeth, that he hath scarcely been able to snatch his ten hours rest at night, much less to employ any portion of his time in contributing to the general amusement. This deponent, however, further saith, that notwithstanding his numerous and indispensable avocations, he hath actually managed to copy each of the said papers, as they have appeared; and in thus having given it his countenance and patronage, he considers himself as entitled to the further indulgence of the court.

The *Affidavit of* Gregory Gripes.

This deponent maketh oath and saith, that ever since the proposals for a newspaper appeared, he has been so grievously afflicted with a pain in his stomach, (which pain doth still continue,) that he has been utterly incapable of contributing any thing towards the support of the said paper; of all which he is ready, if required, to bring into court certificates from the medical men who have attended him. This deponent trusteth that the court will take into its gracious consideration, how impossible it is for a man to attempt to amuse other people, while he himself is labouring under a bodily inconvenience of this peculiar nature.

The Affidavit of Little-care Leave-about.

This deponent maketh oath and saith, that after having more than half-written two or three papers for the Editor's box, some evil-disposed person or persons did, as he believes, during his absence on a walk, steal away from him the said papers, and that he hath never since been able to gain any intelligence of the same.

This deponent furthermore declareth, that such thefts or tricks have been so often practised upon him and his effects, that he doth no longer consider any part of his property safe out of his hands for one moment; nor is his complaint confined to the loss of property alone, but of time also, which is wholly taken up in seeking one stray article after another.

This deponent therefore prayeth the court to take into its most serious consideration the inconvenience both to himself and the public, which results from these proceedings; and that it will be pleased to take such steps as it may, in its wisdom, deem most effectual to prevent the recurrence of the said annoyance.

The Affidavit of Simon Sidrophel.

This deponent maketh oath and saith, that being from the beginning extremely desirous to contribute towards the support of *The Winter Chronicle*, he was determined to search the heavens and the earth for a subject; and therefore betook himself to the study of the globes, in hopes of there stumbling upon something suitable to his purpose. The deponent devoted his first attention to the celestial globe, and earnestly invoked the assistance of every constellation thereupon delineated, but without success. The Great Bear treated him in a manner too rude to be repeated, and the Little Bear (like a dutiful cub,) followed his example. Taurus tossed him, Aries butted

him, and he was thus left sprawling between Castor and Pollux. This malicious pair of rogues pretending friendship, led the deponent on imperceptibly, till he found himself in the claws of Cancer, who pinched him most unmercifully, and determined him to have nothing more to do with the constellations of the Zodiac. Pegasus was the next which appeared, and the deponent, without more ado, resolved to mount him, and at once to enrich the Chronicle by a ride to Parnassus—but this attempt had near cost him his life, for he had scarcely mounted, when Pegasus threw him clean over his head, and dislocated his right shoulder. The deponent being thus scurvily treated in his flight among the stars, had nothing left for it but to return to the Earth. Here he may be said to have traversed the terraqueous globe in search of a subject, but none has yet offered itself. The deponent having made this declaration, leaveth his case to the justice and clemency of the court, conscious that though his name has never yet appeared in the paper, not one of the Contributors has ever gone farther than himself, in search of matter for its support.

The court having latterly testified symptoms of impatience, his lordship motioned the clerk to suspend his reading, and asked the counsellor if he considered the remaining affidavits as containing better reasons than those which the court had already heard. The counsellor answering, " not perhaps better, but some which I trust the court will think equal to the preceding," his lordship directed that the time and patience of the court should no longer be so unnecessarily taken up, and proceeded to give the following judgment :

" That the application for further indulgence be refused, and that the defendants be allowed another week wherein to fulfil the promise made in their name; after which, any further delay was forbidden on pain of the displeasure of the court." TRIM.

THEATRICAL REPORT.

ON Wednesday evening was performed Foote's celebrated comedy of the *Liar*, preceded by a very humorous description of a sea-fight by Mr. Beechey, in the character of a sailor, and which afforded great amusement.

As the Dramatis Personæ have not yet appeared in our paper, we now insert them.

MEN.

Old Wilding,	Mr. NIAS.
Young Wilding,	Captain SABINE.
Papillion,	Mr. BEECHEY.
Sir James Elliot,	Mr. WAKEHAM.

WOMEN.

Miss Grantham,	Mr. Ross.
Miss Godfrey,	Mr. BEVERLEY.
Kitty,	Mr. HOPPNER.

SERVANTS.
Messrs. HALSE and BUSHNAN.

As far as we have been able to learn, this evening's entertainment went off even better than that with which our theatre opened, and was, if possible, received with more rapturous applause.

The *Liar* is a play which requires considerable quickness and animation in the performance; and in this respect so much did the performers appear at home, that we feel confident they may now attempt any play which the theatrical library affords.

It is particularly pleasing to observe the interest which the ships' companies take in these performances; the very preparation of the dresses and scenery in the intervals between them, and of the stage, &c., for two days previous to each play, gives occupation to many: and the looking forward to a repetition of this amusement once a fortnight during the winter, is sure to produce a relaxation and variety which their minds essentially require, and which it might have been difficult to effect in any other way.

A song by Mr. Palmer, between the acts, being the original production of an author who signs himself " Simon Dogrellicus," was well received and encored. We shall content ourselves with repeating our congratulations on the ability, spirit, and good humour, with which our theatrical amusements have hitherto been conducted, and our hearty good wishes for their long and successful continuance.

To the EDITOR *of the* Winter Chronicle.

SIR—In going from the ships towards the observatory the other day, I chanced to stumble on a bundle of papers. On examination, I found them to consist of a number of fragments of letters and other scraps, some in prose, and some in verse, evidently intended to fill some of your future pages, but which want of leisure or inclination had prevented the author from finishing*. As I consider this accident likely to prove a serious loss to your columns, and therefore to the public, unless the papers be returned to the owner in proper time; and, as I know no method of giving them publicity, so effectually as through the medium of your paper for which they were intended, I send you copies of two or three of the fragments, as they lie before me, for insertion if you think proper. Should the lawful owner of the said papers make application to you for them, I

---

* May not this be the identical packet which Mr. Little-care Leave-about conceives to have been stolen from him, (see his Affidavit,) but which may in reality have dropped out of his pocket during his walk?—ED.

will endeavour to stuff the whole bundle by piece-meal into your box, on the first notice you are pleased to give to your constant reader,

RICHARD ROAM-ABOUT.

FRAGMENT, N°. I.

SIR—Having puzzled the little brains I have, to no purpose, for a fortnight, I did at length attempt the other day to scramble unperceived a note into your box; but, after attempting for some minutes to make it fall into the slit, I found, to my utter astonishment, that it refused to drop through, and actually rose again as often as I attempted to thrust it in; so that, after repeated endeavours, I had the mortification to be obliged to withdraw my maiden contribution, on hearing a footstep approaching. I am much at a loss to account for this extraordinary, and to me alarming, phenomenon, unless it be, that in the present cold, and therefore dense, state of the atmosphere, it must, according to the laws of floating bodies, require something of considerable weight to fall into your box; whereas, my production being, as I confess, one of the lightest things imaginable, rose in spite of my endeavours, and would probably, had it not been stopped by the housing, have soared into its own native region, among the clouds. Being much discouraged by this first attempt, I wish any of your learned correspondents, who have instructed us so much on the subject of intense cold and its effects, would give me a hint whether the phenomenon I have alluded to might not have proceeded from some other cause than mere lightness. At all events, should my first apprehensions prove correct, I will endeavour to take example from Philosophicus, Philo-Comus, Philo-Somnus, and the rest of your Philo-correspondents; and have no doubt I shall in time be able to produce something heavy enough to gain admission into your box, and perhaps even to deserve insertion in your pages.

FRAGMENT, N°. II.

ADVERTISEMENT.—In preparation, and shortly will be circulated gratis, for the benefit of all contributors to *The Weekly Chronicle*, and particularly the younger ones, a complete list alphabetically arranged, of the most approved anonymous signatures, adapted to every subject that is likely to employ the pens of the said contributors, by
* * * * * * *

(As the author could not find a signature for this Advertisement, I am afraid this promised list is in no very forward state.)

R. R.

Theatre Royal, North Georgia.

ON WEDNESDAY, DECEMBER 8, 1819, will be Performed the Farce of

THE CITIZEN.

MEN.

Old Philpot, Mr. PARRY.   Sir Jasper Wilding, Mr. NIAS.
Beaufort, Mr. WAKEHAM.   Young Philpot, Mr. BEECHEY.   Young Wilding, Mr. HOPPNER.
Dapper, Mr. GRIFFITHS.   Quilldrive, Mr. BUSHNAN.   Will, Mr. HALSE.

WOMEN.

Maria, Mr. HOOPER.   Corinna, Mr. ROSS.

The usual Accompaniment of Songs between the Acts.

Doors to be opened at Half-past Six, and the Curtain will rise precisely at Seven o'Clock.

THE
NORTH GEORGIA GAZETTE,

PER·FRETA·HACTENUS·NEGATA.

AND
WINTER CHRONICLE.

N°. VI—MONDAY, DECEMBER 9, 1819.

TO THE

EDITOR *of the* WINTER CHRONICLE.

SIR,

A REMARK which appeared in your first Number, that you were willing to " admit questions which may exercise the ingenuity of your readers," &c., has encouraged me to propose one, which, perhaps, may be considered as answering that description. It is said that instances have occurred of the sinking of ice, and this in seas (for example, those of Spitzbergen and Davis' Straits) nearly as salt as the main ocean, and of which the temperature is seldom or never more than ten degrees above the freezing point of salt-water. It is evident that the ice cannot sink till its specific gravity exceed that of the fluid in which it is immersed. I should be glad to be informed by any of your Correspondents, by what possible combination of circumstances so unusual a condition might be brought about.

I am, Mr. Editor,

&c. &c. &c.,

SCEPTICUS.

To the EDITOR *of the* Winter Chronicle.

Mr. EDITOR—I wish you well—indeed I do—but the more I try to compose any thing for the paper, the more stupid I find myself. Being desirous, however, to offer my humble services in some way or other, this is to inform you, that I am a tolerable hand at making pens, though but an indifferent one at using them; and I cannot help thinking, that I might be of use to several of your Correspondents, for I judge by their style, that some of them write with too hard a pen, and some with a very soft one. I could mention three or four, whose cramped manner indicates a dev'lish stiff nib, Mr. Editor, and as many whose pens have certainly no point at all. I confess that the pens of most of your Correspondents require little or no mending, but even the best of them would not be the worse for a fresh nib, which might, perhaps, set them a-going with fresh vigour—so if you choose to employ me in this way, you shall be welcome to the humble services of

TIMOTHY QUILL-SPLITTER.

For the WINTER CHRONICLE.

To the Right Honourable the Lord Chief Justice, and the Worshipful Court of Common Sense, the Memorial of Marmaduke Trim, Reporter of Pleadings, &c. &c.,

Humbly sheweth,

That by the exercise of the said calling, your memorialist hath lived, in good credit and report, until the last week, when your memorialist discovered, in the public papers, a statement of your lordship's decision, purporting to have been taken by himself, in a cause recently pending, before your lordship and this honourable court; whereas, on the day aforesaid, your memorialist was confined at home by urgent business. Your memorialist hath since discovered the decision above-mentioned to have been erroneously stated, as your lordship then declared that defendants were entitled to indulgence, and, in your goodness, were accordingly pleased to grant them such further delay as they might themselves think requisite :

That the said incorrectness, arising, as your memorialist believes, from the reporter leaving the court before the decision was given, is most unjustly attributed to your memorialist; and he finds it, therefore, impossible to vend particular speeches of celebrated counsellors, confessions of prisoners, &c. &c., as heretofore, among his friends, the hawkers, ballad-singers, &c., those gentlemen having taken offence at his supposed want of veracity, and he is, in fact, entirely thrown out of employment.

That these disasters having befallen your memorialist, in consequence of the fictitious use of his name by the said reporter; your memorialist humbly solicits that your lordship will be pleased to affix to the following bill of damages, such sums as your lordship shall consider a sufficient remuneration, and compel the said fictitious Mr. Trim to pay the same, or else to take your memorialist's wife, and six hungry brats, off his hands.

And your Memorialist will ever pray,

&c. &c. &c.

TRIM.

Bill of Damages referred to in the foregoing Memorial.

To a severe fit of head-ach, on receiving news of the said affair.

To a two-hours' lecture from my wife, for daring to be sick without her leave.

To pay of six strong-lunged hawkers, for crying about the " Defence of Reporter Trim," for two days.

To the hire of two female ballad-singers, a bankrupt bellows-mender, and a dog without a tail, roaring a song, called *Trim and Trim's Ghost*, through various streets, lanes, and alleys.

To the loss of forty-eight hours' sleep already, and the probable loss of as many more.

To the cure of a broken nose, two black eyes, and a scratched face, received from my wife, for letting her and the children starve.

To total loss of business, impediments, obstructions, &c. &c., caused by the said fraud.

Advertisements.

WANTED, a middle-aged Woman, not above thirty, of good character, to assist in DRESSING the LADIES at the THEATRE. Her salary will be handsome; and she will be allowed tea and small beer into the bargain. None need apply but such as are perfectly acquainted with the business, and can produce undeniable references.—A line addressed to the Committee will be duly attended to.—N. B. A widow will be preferred.

WANTED immediately, a few BALES of READY WIT, done up in small parcels for the *Winter Chronicle*. This article being scarce in the market, a good price may be depended on. Samples will be received by A. B., Agent to the Editor. Please to apply on or before Thursday evening next.

LOST, on Monday evening last, between the two Ships, a PART of a LETTER, giving an account of the proceedings of the Expedition, with other matters of a private nature, and beginning " My dearest Susan." —Whoever has found the same, is requested to address it, L. A., Editor's box.

N. B. The letter is of no use to any body but the owner.

FOR SALE BY AUCTION,
By NICHOLAS KNOCKDOWN, at the Observatory, on the Coldest Day in January next,

A QUANTITY of NANKEEN, the property of a Gentleman, who expected to get into the Pacific in September last.

₊ Flannels and furs will be gladly taken as part payment.

ACCIDENTS, OFFENCES, &c.

Saturday.—This morning *Canis Vulpes**, a state prisoner, who had been confined in the Barrel, succeeded in effecting his escape, by breaking the chain with which it had been found necessary to secure him, and went off with it appended to his neck. An immediate, though fruitless, pursuit was made, but it is hoped he will not long escape the vigilant eye of our police.

Two P.M.—One of our scouts, Don Carlo †, who has just returned, saw the prisoner in close conference with the proscribed traitor, *Canis Lupus‡*, and his wife; but he so carefully avoided surprise, that the Don had no opportunity of serving the warrant with which he was charged. He gained, however, some important intelligence, having overheard the late prisoner disclosing to his companions the various scenes which he had lately witnessed. He described the cave in which he was confined as inhabited by animals standing upright on their hind legs, who were almost always eating; that notwithstanding their formidable appearance, he believed them to be a very timid race; for that, every morning, he saw a great many of these creatures meet together, and all at once, upon hearing a sharp shrill noise §, which he thought was made by some other animal they stood in great terror of, they ran away and hid themselves in another cave they had under the first; and he strongly insisted on it, that this noise was not half so terrific as that of *Canis Lupus*. His spleen was, however, more particularly directed against one which he supposed was

---

* A fox escaped from the Griper on that day.
† A dog named Carlo.
‡ Wolves were often seen about the ships during the winter.
§ The boatswain piping to breakfast.

a cub, who had not yet learned to walk upright, as he always went on all fours; his spite arose, he said, from this little creature making faces and growling, and doing all he could to annoy him, whenever he put his head out of the hole in the side of his cave. The conference ended by a mutual agreement to seize this unfortunate animal, as soon as opportunity offered, from whom they expected to learn more of the prowess and habits of their new foes; and for this purpose a variety of stratagems were proposed, which will probably be put in execution.

For the WINTER CHRONICLE.

A THOUGHT OF HOME.

LOVELY Woman's the pride of our Isle,
  With Beauty's soft image imprest,
Fondly raptured we gaze on her smile,
  To harmony soothing the breast!
The rose-bud's young opening dye,
  And the lily's pure vesture she wears;
But the love-beaming glance of her eye,
  With lilies nor roses compares.

Bounteous Nature her flow'rets may paint
  With tinctures of azure and gold,
Yet their lustre shines dimly and faint,
  Till sun-beams their splendour unfold:
So the mild dawning virtues that dwell
  In a bosom enchantingly fair,
Bid that bosom more beauteously swell
  The woes of another to share.

In those virtues we happiness feel;
  The source of our transport below,
Not the charms of the sex can reveal;
  From the mind, soul-enchantment must flow.
When sorrows intrude on our peace,
  When wrung by anxiety's wound,
Her endearments procure us release;
  How sweet is her tenderness found!

Man is gifted with firmness of mind,
  In dangers and triumphs to share,
But each beauty and softness combined,
  Distinguish the lovely and fair;
All the soul-winning graces and loves
  On Britain's fair footsteps attend;
And when Beauty too transient removes
  With the Virtues, above, they shall blend.

For the WINTER CHRONICLE.

———

" Come write for the paper," the Editor cries,
　'Tis Thursday—my box has no stuffing."
Egad then your box, as at present it lies,
　Is just like my head, a mere puffin !
I have not one jot, or one atom of brain,
　At this present moment of writing ;
And whilst I so dreadfully stupid remain,
　'Tis nonsense to think of inditing.
Should a smart witty thought ever happen to light,
　By design or by chance on my skull,
You, then, may rely on't I'll instantly write,
　And just give you the subject in full.
LITTLE-BRAIN LACK-WIT.

———

REFLECTIONS ON SEEING THE SUN SET FOR A PERIOD OF THREE MONTHS.
NOVEMBER, 1819.

———

Behold yon glorious orb, whose feeble ray
Mocks the proud glare of Summer's livelier day !
His noon-tide beam shot upward thro' the sky,
Scarce gilds the vault of Heaven's blue canopy—
A fainter yet, and yet a fainter light—
And lo ! he leaves us now to one long cheerless night !

And is his glorious course for ever o'er ?
And has he set indeed—to rise no more ?
To us no more shall Spring's enlivening beam,
Unlock the fountains of the fetter'd stream—
No more the wild bird carol through the sky,
And cheer yon mountains with rude melody ?—

*　*　*　*　*　*　*　*　*　*

Once more shall Spring her energy resume,
And chase the horrors of this wintry gloom—
Once more shall Summer's animating ray
Enliven Nature with perpetual day—
Yon radiant orb, with self-inherent light
Shall rise, and dissipate the shades of night,
In peerless splendour re-possess the sky,
And shine in renovated majesty

In yon departing orb methinks I see
A counterpart of frail mortality.
Emblem of man! when life's declining sun
Proclaims this awful truth, " Thy race is run !"
His sun once set—its bright effulgence gone,
All, all is darkness—as it ne'er had shone !

Yet not *for ever* is man's glory fled,
His name for ever ' numbered with the dead'—
Like yon bright orb, th' immortal part of man
Shall end in glory, as it first began,—
Like Him, encircled in celestial light,
Shall rise triumphant midst the shades of night,
Her native energies again resume,
Dispel the dreary winter of the tomb,
And, bidding Death with all its terrors fly,
Bloom in perpetual Spring thro' all eternity !

THE
NORTH GEORGIA GAZETTE,

PER·FRETA·HACTENUS·NEGATA·

AND
WINTER CHRONICLE.

N°. VII—MONDAY, DECEMBER 13, 1819.

Mr. Editor,

THOUGH I have not the pleasure of your personal acquaintance, yet the favourable impression I have received of your humanity when you interfered to save me from the tonsorial operation recommended by Philosophicus, emboldens me to apply to you for advice in a case where not only my hair, but skin, carcass and all are in danger, amidst the horrors of Winter, of being reduced to ashes.

You must know then, Sir, that a certain gentleman, (whom I will not describe to you as a sedate looking sort of a man, with a thin face, and so on, because that might seem to result from ill-nature,)—this gentleman I say, Sir, takes particular delight, when I am sleeping before the fire, in putting a hot cinder under my thigh, and then laughs most heartily to see me run away, holding it fast, from the sense of pain, until I am fully awake. Now, Sir, I have endured this and similar tricks for some time, and, though often meditating retaliation, I dare not execute it, as the result of biting his legs, besides perhaps breaking my teeth against the bones, would be banishment from the fire-side, and I would submit to any indignity rather than forfeit so great an advantage.

I dare say you participate somewhat in my feelings; but to put the case more strongly, suppose, Mr. Editor, some wight, when you were sunk in sound repose, should clap a hot coal under you! Now, this was just my case the other night; and, as I am a poor helpless innocent, if you can inform me how I can obtain revenge, consistently with my interest, or escape the future persecution of my tormentor, you will confer a deep obligation on   Pincher.

THEATRE ROYAL NORTH GEORGIA.

———

On Wednesday evening, the Farce of *The Citizen* was played with a spirit and success fully equalling the expectations to which the former performances at this theatre had given rise. We cannot omit to notice especially the animation and effect with which the very difficult scene was carried through, in which Old Philpot is discovered under the table in Corinna's lodgings; during all this scene the house was kept in continual laughter.

Two songs were introduced at intervals—the well-known one of "Arthur O'Bradley," by Mr. Beechey, and a new song written for the occasion, and sung by Mr. Palmer, to the tune of "The Bay of Biscay O."

———

Theatre Royal, North Georgia.

———

On Thursday, December 23, 1819, will be performed Garrick's celebrated Farce of

THE MAYOR OF GARRATT.

MEN.

Sir Jacob Jollup,   Mr. Nias.   Major Sturgeon, Mr. Bushnan.

    Jerry Sneak, Mr. Beechey.   Bruin, Mr. Wakeham.

    Crispin Heeltap, Mr. Hulse.   Matthew Mug, Mr. Parry.

        Lint, Mr. Beverley.   Snuffle, Mr. Griffiths.

WOMEN.

Mrs. Sneak, Mr. Hooper.   Mrs. Bruin, Mr. Ross.

        Mob, &c. &c.

After which will be represented, an entire new Musical Entertainment, written expressly for the occasion, called,

THE NORTH-WEST PASSAGE;

OR,

THE VOYAGE FINISHED.

MEN.

Seamen of the Hecla.

Tom, Mr. Nias.   Harry, Mr. Griffiths.   Bill, Mr. Palmer.

Seamen of the Griper.

Jack, Mr. Hoppner.   Dick, Mr. Wakeham.

Landlord, Mr. Bushnan.   Brother to Susan, Mr. Hulse.   An Esquimaux, Mr. Hulse.

WOMEN.

Susan, Mr. Hooper.   Poll, Mr. Ross.

Doors will be opened at Half past Six, and the Curtain will rise at Seven o'Clock precisely.

Advertisements.

WANTS a PLACE, a Gentleman, who will undertake to write DOGGREL VERSES for the THEATRE or NEWSPAPER. Will contract to write by the foot, yard, or fathom.

Please to apply to O. P., next door to Q.'s Printing Office. No connexion with Simon Doggrellicus, Albert, or Q.

WANTED, for the use of the Performers, a considerable PORTION of ASSURANCE; also a quantity of sound retentive memory, (for repairs) at per yard. Any gentleman possessing a superabundance of these requisites will be treated with on liberal terms. Apply to the Committee.

AN Amateur is desirous of procuring a GOOD VOICE, with instructions for its management.

Application to be made at the Club Room, Pipe-street, prior to Christmas Eve.

A CELEBRATED Literary Character has procured, during an excursion among the Stars, some very BRIGHT IDEAS, which he means to submit to the inspection of his friends and the public, in the course of the ensuing week.

A GENTLEMAN, labouring under the inconvenience of an increasing corporation, would give his VOTE and INTEREST at the next CITY ELECTION to any person removing the complaint without a reduction of diet.

Particulars may be obtained at the Pump Room, Bath.

LOST, Stolen, or Strayed, a WHITE FOX, with a long tail and a longer chain; answers to the name of Jack. As he must be somewhere on the island, or on the ice in its immediate neighbourhood, he may easily be found.

Address to G. R. No. 2, North Georgia.

A GENTLEMAN, who has endeavoured to beguile the tedious wintry hours in practising some pieces of music, presented to him by a fair and much esteemed friend, having been peculiarly unfortunate in breaking the strings of his violin, wishes to purchase ONE of the FELINE SPECIES, in order to replace them.

Inquiry to be made at the Academy of Arts and Sciences.

LEFT, behind the scenes, after the performance, on Wednesday evening, a BOX, containing a parcel of comfits, two bottles of lavender water, a small packet of rouge, some white powder, five artificial teeth, one pair of eye-brows, three large mustachios, with whiskers to correspond; sixteen papers of court plaster, a silver thimble, marked E. R., a pair of ladies' garters, seven gold rings, with various stones, one having the device of two hearts transfixed with an arrow, three smelling bottles, a pin-cushion, a pair of curling-irons, several bottles of rose-water, and various other perfumes; with a number of smaller articles, among which is a recipe for promoting the growth of a beard.

The owner may have it again, by describing the box, on application at the Green-room of the Theatre.

To the Editor of the Winter Chronicle.

SIR—I beg to correct an error which has crept into the third page of your last Number, under the head of accidents, offences, &c. The prison from which the state prisoner therein mentioned made his escape, was not the *Barrel*, but the *Fleet*

Yours, &c.

PITIFUL PUNSTER, *Bart.*

For the WINTER CHRONICLE.

THE GREEN-ROOM, OR A PEEP BEHIND THE CURTAIN.

I.

COME list to a story my Muse would relate,
    A story she long will remember,
To tell it in verse, she has puzzled her pate;
'Tis a scene that occurred in North Georgia—late
    One evening in gloomy December.

II.

'Twas night, and the moon had illumined the hill,
  Not a leaf on the mountain-top trembled,
The wolf ceased his howling, and each purling rill
Had forgotten to murmur, as frozen streams will,
Not a sound could be heard, for all nature stood still,
  While the players in the green-room assembled!

III.

First old Daddy Philpot * came tottering in,
  As tall and as stiff as a hop-stick,
With woe-begone visage, lank chops and long chin,
He for all the world look'd like the picture of Sin,
  Or like a Death's head on a mop-stick !

IV.

" Adzooks !" quoth Maria *, " this body won't meet;
  " How the deuce shall I e'er get my sash on ?
" These shoes are too clumsy by half for my feet—
" So do what I will I shall never look neat,
  " It 's enough to put Job in a passion !"

V.

Then comes the young Cit *, in his coat of light green,
  (*Nota bene*, 'twas made of a curtain,)
Like a true city counting-house dandy, I ween :
Such a medley of finery never was seen,
  At this end of the town, I am certain.

VI.

" You Tom," cries Corinna, " come lace up my stays,
  " But tuck my shirt carefully first in."
Tom pull'd till Corinna look'd red in the face,
But she bore it, sweet soul, with a very good grace,
When, bounce ! went an eye-let hole, crack went the lace,
  'Twas like a ripe gooseberry bursting !

VII.

Then enter poor Beaufort, with look so profound,
  You 'd have sworn he was troubled with phthisic ;
" You look, sir," quoth Moll, " like a sheep in a pound,
" Or a soldier afloat, or a sailor aground,
  " Or a monkey about to take physic ! †"

Characters in the *Citizen*, which was preparing for representation.
† " I like a simile half a mile long."—*Maria* in the *Citizen*.

VIII.

And here my poor Muse is in utter despair,
   To record half the pother unable,
Such bustle and racket, and uproar were there,
She cannot find ought that may with it compare ;
Yet, stay—was you ever at Bart'lemy fair ?
   'Twas a downright theatrical Babel.

IX.

" You've laced me so tight, I declare I'm half dead,"
   " Pooh, nonsense, make haste, put your shoes on.
" Where the devil's my wig ?"—" Why, a top of your head."
" Who can lend me a pin, or a needle and thread?
" I wish it was over, and I snug in bed."
   Happy scene of theatric confusion !

X.

But see ! the confusion draws near to a close,
   And the Muse has near done her inditing.
The painter his art on each visage bestows ;
By skilful arrangement on many a nose
The-lily now blooms, where before blush'd the rose.
   Good luck to vermilion and whiting !

XI.

Hark ! hark ! 'tis the prompter, whose magical bell
   Makes the stoutest heart feel palpitation !
I shall not detain you, kind reader, to tell
How *this* one played passably, *that* very well,
With other important events that befel
   The *Dram. Pers.* on this merry occasion !

XII.

Yet lest you should fancy my Muse meant to teaze,
   Be this the last verse of her story !
Long, long, may their efforts continue to please,
And long may Old England have actors like these,
And ships to conduct them across the proud seas,
   To add a new wreath to her glory.

PEEPING TOM.

THE

NORTH GEORGIA GAZETTE,

AND

WINTER CHRONICLE.

Nº. VIII—MONDAY, DECEMBER 20, 1819.

TO THE

EDITOR *of the* WINTER CHRONICLE.

SIR,

IN looking over some old manuscript sea-journals, which were bequeathed to me by my grand-father, and which I had never till now leisure or curiosity to examine, I find an imperfect one which seems to relate to an attempt very similar to that in which we are now engaged. The date is uncertain, the second and most material figure of the year being unfortunately erased thus " A.D. 1-19." Thinking, however, that it may amuse some of your readers if inserted in your paper, I transcribe all that is legible :

" ——— So seeing wee might make no more progresse this yeare, wee did counselle to come to lande if a haven there might be found, for winter-securitie; and having searched diligentlie for yᵉ same, by God's goodnesse, and our pilot's skille in marine affaires, we came to anchor in a goodlie bay, where by divers goode observations we did find the height of yᵉ Northern Pole near seventie-and-five degrees.

Here wee did abide about nine months, and having good store of provisions (beside deere and other meate that wee did kille) we wanted for nothing but employment in this our icy prisonne, and that our companie might not runne into mischief, for lack of hilaritie, wee did contrive sundrie jocose plans for our merrie-making, insomuch that his Highnesse the Devil could never gaine the ascendancie. But there were three or foure amongst our companie (who as wee did conceive did entertaine secret communication with his Worshippe) who willed not to joyne with us in this our hilaritie, albeit they did not fail to benefitte therebye without any pains by them taken. Thereupon, our captaine, observing the same, did justlie order them to be shortlie provisioned, like men in a garrisonne who will not fight the enemie, ' for' said he ' those which do not benefitte the communitie, the communitie is not bounden to benefitte *them.*' So they're choppes grew more leane than ordinairie, and likewise theyre legges which caused *them* to wax exceeding wrath, and *us* exceeding merrie. Albeit, our companie nothing heeding theyre indignation, did cause theyre cheekes to be singed with a red-hotte ironne, fashioned after the letters N. C. (whose meaning, being no scholar, i could not fathome) by which our friendes in Old Englande might aske and know theyre historie. After this fashion wee did turne theyre inactivitie to our own merrimente, and did so compasse the Devil and his Impes, by turning theyre own weapones againest them ————."

It is much to be regretted that no more of this curious manuscript is legible; for, the old navigator seem to have been placed in a situation so exactly similar to ours, that I doubt not we might have received many useful hints from their experience, in addition to those I have transcribed.

I am, Mr. Editor,
Your obedient Servant,
T.

To the EDITOR of the Winter Chronicle.

SIR—I regret to acquaint you, that in consequence of the chief justice having ruptured a blood-vessel in a violent fit of laughter, occasioned by seeing Counsellor Puzzlewell enter the hall with a conical paper cap on, fantastically ornamented with small bells, the Court of Common Sense is at present closed. The period of its re-opening has not yet been determined on.

OBSERVER.

Advertisement.

To the MANAGER and COMMITTEE of the Theatre Royal, North Georgia.

GENTLEMEN—I am a widow, twenty-six years of age, and can produce undeniable testimonials of my character and qualifications; but before I undertake the business of dressing the ladies at the theatre, I wish to be informed whether it is customary for them to keep on their breeches; also, if I may be allowed two or three of the stoutest able-seamen or marines, to lace their stays. So no more at present from,

Gentlemen, yours as may be,
ABIGAIL HANDICRAFT.

P. S. Could you allow hollands instead of beer? As for tea, that is no object.

To the EDITOR of the North Georgia Gazette.

SIR—As I was yesterday indulging in a fit of somnolency, or in other words, dozing before the fire-side, a sort of waking dream presented itself to my fancy, which I beg the liberty of detailing. I thought I was in one of the cabins, observing the operations of a gentleman in the next to it, through a chink in the bulk-head. He was sitting at a table facing me, and I soon discovered " the poet's eye in a fine frenzy rolling." He had a sheet of paper before him, on which his hand unconsciously wandered with a slower or more rapid motion, as the bright ideas seemed to float on his intellectual sight. After a pause of a few moments he began, but I must ever regret that the tone, the energy of the voice, the expression of the dark eye, the fierce animation of the countenance, cannot be conveyed by words. He began as follows :

" The moon, resplendent orb, I ween
" Shone brilliant, like————

" Like, like, let me see—I have it

" ———————— like our soup tureen ;
" The shaggy wolf stalked on the shore
" Like,

" Like what ? for I must have another simile —boatswains—no, no, he's too dark—stop I can remedy that—

" Like boatswain daub'd with lime or flour.
" The stars half quench'd, seemed scattered there
" Like bristles on ———'s chin.
" While in the hollow ships we lie."

" That line's good, but useless; unless I get some lofty shining touch every two or three lines, these epics go for nothing. One's comparisons should be natural, striking, easily flowing into the verse. Such a one has just popped into my head, and I'll go over it once again.

" While in the hollow ships we lie,
" Like pears or blackbirds in a pie ;
" Or like that fish so much renown'd,
" That on the Cornish coast is found
" A Pilchard hight—who same as we
" Peeps through the crust, the stars to see."

Judge my disappointment, Mr. Editor, when the dinner-bell ringing, started the poet from his reverie ! But, if before his features glowed with Achillean fire, they now assumed the glare of the hungry tiger ; and, I doubt if the latter would have outdone his speed in reaching the dinner-table. I need hardly add, that the same bell which called my friend away, put an end to the delusion, by awaking me.

I am, Sir, your sincere well-wisher,

PHILO-SOMNUS.

———————

Philo-Somnus's letter reached us last week, but our columns did not admit of its insertion ; since which, a circumstance has occurred which makes us consider the delay as especially fortunate. We regarded his communication simply as a *jeu-d'esprit*, without a suspicion that it had its foundation in reality. We were most agreeably surprised, therefore, on receiving during the present week the effusions of the poet whom Philo-Somnus overheard in the act of composition, completed for our pages such as we now subjoin them. Philo-Somnus's letter, however, is not the less interesting ; it may remind some of our readers of the pleasure with which they have read the original draft of Mr. Pope's translation of the *Iliad*, as compared with the finished and published copy.

———————

TO THE

EDITOR *of the* WINTER CHRONICLE.

———

Mr. EDITOR,

If the following efforts of my Muse should be deemed worthy a place in your valuable columns, their insertion will afford much gratification to,

A YOUNG BEGINNER.

THE moon, resplendent orb, shines bright I ween,
Its brilliance is just like our soup tureen.
The snow-drift, wafted by the passing breeze,
Looks like that vessel fill'd with boiling pease,
That thrice each week smokes fragrant on our board
In shape of soup, pea-soup, to feed the horde.
The shaggy wolf stalks slowly on the shore,
 Like boatswain when with hoar-frost cover'd o'er.
The stars shine dimly, and seem scatter'd thin,
Just like the bristles seen on ————'s chin,
 Like leaves in spring, when trees begin their budding,
Or like the plums stuck in our Sunday's pudding.
While in the hollow ships we snugly lie
Like blackbirds—or black-berries in a pie ;
Or like that fish so long, so much renown'd,
That on the Cornish coast in swarms abound,
A pilchard hight, who, quite as snug as we,
Peeps through the crust, the moon and stars to see;
And hence, by people, keen and sharp as razors,
Have they, as we, been oft-times call'd star-gazers.
We muster twice on each revolving day,
Like shepherds who take care their flocks don't stray.
We keep a watch by night, I'd have you know,
But then 'tis like a watch that does not go.
We take each meal at its accustom'd hour,
What hunger once made sweet, but now tastes sour.
Our appetites have left us, much like those
From whom pale sickness steals away health's rose :
But not like those we sleep—for, know, we snore
Like men who knew not how to sleep before.
Thus do we watch, eat, drink, and sleep amain,
And then, we watch, eat, drink, and sleep again.

—To drive this dull monotony away,
Once every fortnight we get up a play ;
Delightful bustle, each face wears a smile,
There's nought like plays dull *tædium* to beguile ;
With Spring's return, I trust they'll still be found
A record how good humour may abound ;
And shew that men, who take the proper course,
May always in themselves find such resource,
As to ensure of care the banishment,
And shew how much depends on management.
With Spring's return, like the industrious bee,
Behold all bustle, all activity !
At Spring's return, when Phœbus shews his head,
Like Sluggard rising from his feather-bed,

We'll shake dull sloth and indolence away,
And give our minds no longer to a play.
Fired with fresh ardour, and with bold intent,
Our minds shall, like our prows, be westward bent,
Until Pacific's waves pour forth sweet sounds,
Chiming to us like—*Twenty thousand pounds!*

To the EDITOR *of the* Winter Chronicle.

SIR—At first sight of your correspondent *P's* rebus inserted in your fifth number, I gave myself credit for having at once discovered the solution ; but the *two-fifths* of the first article destroyed my airy hope, until by chance a day or two since I met with a seaman's letter, wherein his dear Sally expresses an earnest hope that her letter will reach him in the enjoyment of good *Helth*. Now, Sir, as I consider Mr. P. has possibly learned to spell out of the same dictionary with Sally, I shall no longer hesitate in laying before you the score of lines which I have eked out, in elucidation of the author's meaning.

I am, &c. &c.,

CASTIGATOR.

SOLUTION.

ON the wave or on the shore,
Nobly born or humbly poor,
Blest with competence or wealth
Man's first wish must still be *helth ;*
What on monarchs' thrones can shine,
Fair as *Clemency* divine?
Who could with *Adonis* vie,
Peerless in a Goddess' eye ?
If the parts of these you join,
In the word you thus combine,
You 'll a vessel's name disclose
Dreaded oft by Britain's foes * ;
Now commission'd to explore
Unknown seas to Asia's shore ;
And in this unpeopled isle,
Tho' the fact may make you smile,
Doubtless *all* their ship admire,
Seated round her winter fire.
Loudly sound thy trumpet, Fame,
Say, the *Hecla* is her name.

---

* The Hecla's last service, as a ship of war, was as one of Lord Exmouth's fleet, at the attack on Algiers.

THE
NORTH GEORGIA GAZETTE,

PER·FRETA·HACTENUS·NEGATA

AND

WINTER CHRONICLE.

Nº. IX—MONDAY, DECEMBER 27, 1819.

To the EDITOR *of the* Winter Chronicle.

> " He snuffs far off the anticipated joy,
> " Turtle and venison all his thoughts employ,
> " Prepares for meals, as jockeys take a sweat,
> " Oh, nauseous! an emetic for a whet!"

MR. EDITOR,

HAPPENING to stumble a day or two ago upon the above lines, they brought to my recollection an advertisement that I read in your Chronicle last week, dated from the Pump-room, Bath. Notwithstanding the address, however, I suspect from the style of the gentleman, that he is better acquainted in a well-known city somewhat to the eastward; but that is a matter of little import to me, my aim not being so much to gain the no common reward which he holds forth, as to give a freedom to the overflowings of the milk of human kindness, with which my nature (with modesty be it spoken,) is too full. I cannot, however, proceed without making a strong protest against those false and squeamish feelings of the poet, which prompt him to nauseate, or affect to nauseate, the really harmless means which the subject of his rhymes adopted for the attainment of a praiseworthy and voluptuous end; a means too so innocent as to have been practised for time immemorial by many a worthy citizen, without so much as a wry face, still less dreaming of the least indelicacy, in a practice that administered so much delightful sensation. But these poets, Mr. Editor, have been so pampered with high seasoned viands, that it is almost impossible to find food or physic of a material nature sufficiently refined to suit the exquisite sensibility of their appetites. Instead of feeding like other good souls upon turtle or venison, they have fed on ambrosia with the gods. Instead of good old port, they must have nectar, and rejecting Calvert's fine brown-stout, and Meux's entire, nothing forsooth will serve them but gulping down whole streams at the foot of Parnassus. Setting aside, therefore, any attempt to please such dainty gentlemen, I shall leave them to their prejudices, and proceed to offer my advice to the gentleman of the Pump-room. In the first place, let him set the poets at defiance; and in the next commence a course of what the latter has been pleased to call "nauseous," but which the alderman found so useful as a preparative; he however sat

> " Abdominous and wan,
> " Like a fat squab upon a Chinese fan."

Now, I presume it is the idea of this picture that haunts the imagination of our citizen of the Pump-room, the evils of which he foresaw and justly deprecates. Certainly it seems a melancholy prospect, but happily for him, I can place within his grasp the means of contravening such a calamity. I shall endeavour to imitate the skilful physician, and point out how that which was a bane to the one, may be rendered an antidote to the other. My plan, Mr. Editor, has simplicity to recommend it, a quality by which it is distinguished from regular medical practice in general; it consists merely in the trifling inversion of the order of meals and medicines. The alderman took his dose as a preparative, always *before* his meals: let the Pump-room citizen, then, whose object is so different, only get his food first, and take his dose regularly an hour afterwards. And, as long as he shall persevere in the plan, I will readily stake all my credit upon its efficacy.   I am, Sir, &c. &c.,

Philanthropus.

THEATRICAL REPORT.

Thursday evening's entertainment commenced with *The Mayor of Garratt*; a farce which notwithstanding its characters are drawn from low and vulgar life, has ever maintained its popularity by its abundant humour, and by its pointed satire of extensive application. We are of opinion that in none of the preceding performances at this theatre have the characters generally been so well sustained; a circumstance which we are pleased in ascribing to the increased acquaintance of the dramatis personæ with the manners and customs of the stage.

The Mayor of Garratt was followed by a new musical after-piece, the joint production of our principal bards and wits, entitled *The North West Passage*, or *the Voyage Finished*. The characters having been already announced in the advertisement of last Monday se'nnight, and the subject of the piece being obvious from its title, we proceed to give a short account of it. It is divided into five acts for the sake of convenience. The scene of the first is laid at Winter Harbour, and the time is that period to which we so anxiously look forward, *viz.*, when the season of active exertion is recommencing; the Hecla's boat lands, and meets the Griper's sailors on shore; they speak of their future prospects, and many jokes are passed on the transactions of the winter. The act concludes with an appropriate song, and three cheers on leaving Winter Harbour. The second act is supposed to take place early in the summer of 1820, when the ships have succeeded in passing the meridian of Mackenzie's River. Here the same crews meet on the ice, congratulate each other on having gained the second prize, and cheer on to Behring's Straits. During the conversation a bear which is supposed to have been seen in the morning, being allured by the burning of some whales' flesh, appears in the distance chased by a boat which is observed to fire at it. The men secrete themselves, and the bear re-appears in the distance but a little nearer, and at length comes on the stage, where the kettle containing the fish had been left for the purpose of attracting him; after a short encounter, in which one of the Hecla's sailors receives a hug, the bear is killed and carried off. During this act the ships are seen in the distance under sail, and at the conclusion of a song, on a signal of recall being hoisted and a gun fired, the boat pushes off. In the third act the scene changes to Deptford, where Poll and Susan, the sweethearts of Tom and Dick, are discovered sitting at work, and expressing their anxious alarms for the safety of their lovers, of whom no tidings have as yet been received. They are joined by their brother, who produces a newspaper, containing information which the government had obtained from the master of the Brunswick whaler, from the particulars of which, and the circumstance that this was the only vessel by whom the Discovery Ships had been seen in the summer of 1819, the best hopes are augured of their safety and success. In act the fourth we return to the expedition, having now, (i. e., in the autumn of 1820,) reached the so anxiously-desired Behring's Strait. Here nautical congratulations, and the prospects of the *Voyage Finished* occupy them, until their attention is called off by an Esquimaux sledge seen in the distance, and subsequently by the Esquimaux himself, where a scene occurs which brought to our recollection the most interesting event of the expedition of discovery which preceded the present. After making friends with him, by presents and a song, the sailors induce him to accompany them on board. In the fifth and concluding act the scene shifts again to Deptford; the voyage being now finished, the sailors are met at the Prince of Wales, where heartily welcomed by the landlord and joined by their sweethearts, they talk over the difficulties they have passed through, and the good fortune they have enjoyed, and the act concludes with " God save the King" and three cheers, in which the audience most heartily joined.

We shall only add, that the piece produced in its fullest extent the interest and entertainment which were designed. We are all witnesses how much the ship's company participated in these feelings, but it is not easy perhaps fully to appreciate the permanent impression which such representations as these are calculated to establish in their minds.

Theatre Royal, North Georgia.

ON THURSDAY, JANUARY 6, 1820,

When will be performed the celebrated Farce of

BON TON ;

Or, HIGH LIFE ABOVE STAIRS.

MEN.

Lord Minnikin,	Captain Sabine.	Sir John Trotley,	Mr. Parry.
Colonel Tivy,	Mr. Ross,	Jessamy,	Mr. Griffiths.
Davy,	Mr. Nias.	Mignon,	Mr. Bushnan.

WOMEN.

Lady Minikin, Mr. Beechey.   Miss Tittup, Mr. Hooper.   Gymp, Mr. Beverley.

SONGS will be introduced between the Acts.

The Doors to be opened at Half-past Six, and the Curtain will rise precisely at Seven o'Clock

To the Editor *of the* Winter Chronicle.

———

Sir—The Committee beg you to insert the enclosed in your Paper, for which they will feel greatly obliged.

I am, Sir, *&c.,*
SNIP QUILL-DRIVE,
Secretary to the Committee.

To Mrs. Abigail Handicraft.

My dear Madam—The Committee having sat for a considerable time upon your letter, published in last week's Paper, beg me to acquaint you, that the contents have penetrated each member *au fond;* that they feel sore at the prospect of losing your services at the theatre, which they fear will be the case, when you are informed that the gentlemen say that they can't perform their ladies' parts properly with their can't-mention-ums on. The Committee, however, hope that this will not prevent you from accepting the office.

They desire me to add, that two stout able seamen shall attend you with marline-spikes, levers, and white-line; and that gin, instead of beer, at your request, will be allowed, upon promise that you give not a drop to the actresses, as the consequences, you must be aware, may greatly retard the performances of the piece.

I have the honour to be, Madam, *&c.,*
S. QUILL-DRIVE, *Sec.*

Advertisements.

———

LOST, either in the Pit or Lobby of the Theatre, on Thursday last, a SMALL MEMORANDUM BOOK, containing notes and strictures on the new entertainment; also remarks, on the merits of the respective performers, made on the spot, and calculated to afford hints for an elaborate criticism on the above subjects, intended to form an Appendix to the Writer's Journal, which will be published on the return of the Expedition.—Whoever has found the same, and will return it to No. 3, Link-lane, will be handsomely rewarded for their trouble.

AN Amateur, who has generally had female characters assigned to him, is desirous of receiving a FEW HINTS on the most becoming attitudes, actions, and articulations, for a Woman of Fashion; also, on the most approved method of obtaining the fashionable stoop, without appearing round-shouldered.

Application to be made at No. 2, Ordnance-square.

THIS is to give Notice, that a couple of FINE CALVES have, within the last week, been *grazed* by Deal Board, Carpenter, who resides at the foot of Hatchway Passage, and that they were carried away from thence by a stout man, to be dressed; but it was supposed that they would produce more *woe* than *weal* to the thief, as they were thought to be the identical Calves that had strayed from No. 1, Bell-lane.

SONG FROM THE NORTH-WEST PASSAGE.

WRITTEN BY MR. WAKEHAM,

AND SUNG BY MR. PALMER.

———

I.

When a ship boy at first on the ocean's rude wave,
I was taught to disdain ev'ry thought of a slave,
Bold freedom to nurture, that valour inspires,
And proves England's tars still are worthy their sires.

II.

As to manhood I grew, and a sailor became,
Ev'ry hope, ev'ry wish of my heart was the same;
My Susan, my parents, but strengthened the claim,
I knew that their bliss must depend on my fame.

III.

Stern war was gone by, and our ensigns no more
Waved proudly triumphant o'er each hostile shore ;
But I heard of two ships that were fitting to seek
For new lands in the North, where the winds bellow bleak.

IV

My bosom was fired, and I soon was enroll'd
In the fortunate band, for adventure so bold,
Whom I now see before me resolved to maintain
That their country shall never call on them in vain.

V.

And say if privations or perils should rise,
Why what would they weigh in a true seaman's eyes ?
He'd scorn the base thought of e'er turning his back,
His hand ever ready—his heart never slack.

VI.

If one dastard like this !—no—such one there can't be
In these ships that have dash'd thro' this ice-fettered sea !
Then may those who act nobly—as all of you will,
Safe returned, have of love and of pleasure their fill.

VII.

May the Butcher and Bull, Prince of Wales, and each port
Where the Hecla's and Griper's incline to resort,
Abound with good liquor, with fiddles and song,
And plenty of lasses to cheer up the throng.

For the WINTER CHRONICLE.

REFLECTIONS ON THE MORNING OF CHRISTMAS DAY, 1819, NORTH GEORGIA.

Rich from the blushing East no glory darts
To chase the shadowy night ;—but all is gloom,
Save where the moon's young crescent o'er the snows
Emits a trembling radiance, faintly seen
Through mists obscure ;—or sparkling seen on high
The countless myriads of the stars diffuse
Their distant, glimmering, scarce-enlightening rays !
Behind yon cloud a stream of paly light*

* Aurora Borealis.

Shoots up its pointed spires—again immerged,
Sweeps forth with sudden start, and waving round
In changeful forms, assumes the brighter glow
Of orient topaz—then as sudden sinks
In deeper russet, and at once expires!

Here then we view, in Northern Isle immured
Midst ceaseless drifts and long-enduring ice
The wonder of His pow'r, whose awful voice
Spoke earth into existence, and the sun
That now, Britannia! o'er thy favour'd land
Lights up the day thro' winter's cheerless reign.

Hail, sacred hours! that to my mind recal
His wondrous goodness.   His, the Great Supreme!
Once was thy morn in other splendour drest,
When to the shepherd-train's astonish'd eyes
Celestial glory shone, and angel choirs
Hymn'd the Messiah's birth in songs divine!
And shall not man prolong the wondrous strain,
For whom this mightiest, greatest work was done?
Yes, whether bord'ring on the Icy Pole,
Or where the genial ray with fruits and flow'rs
Bedecks the pendant bough, or paints the vale,
Still let the hymn of triumph rise on high,
The hymn of grateful joy incessant rise
To Jesu's name, our Saviour and our God!
Who laid his glory by, and wrapt in flesh
Our natures shared, exempt alone from sin,
For purposes of love; to save mankind,
To raise us to a higher state of bliss
Than in primeval innocence enjoy'd
Our great progenitor—fruition pure,
Eternal, full, unmeasurable joy!
Still as expiring years shall roll along
Be this our theme, when wintry skies proclaim
This sacred day's return : and higher thoughts
Than sordid pleasures fill our tongues with praise,
Our hearts with love, our bosoms with desire
To live to Him who gave His life for us,
While yet we are on Earth; and when at length
The hour that frees th' imprison'd soul shall come,
Calm, may we view the stern approach of Death
But parting from a world of painful toil
To dwell for ever near Jehovah's throne!
To whom be glory, pow'r, dominion, praise,
Ascribed for ever, and for evermore!

THE
NORTH GEORGIA GAZETTE,

PER · FRETA · HACTENUS · NEGATA

AND
WINTER CHRONICLE.

Nº. X.—MONDAY, JANUARY 3, 1820.

To the Editor *of the* Winter Chronicle.

Winter Harbour, North Georgia,
Satur day, Jan.1, 1820.

Sɪʀ,

Iᴛ has always appeared to me, that the frequent recurrence of the various holydays and festivals ordained by the Church, independently of the important events which they are intended to commemorate, may be considered as contributing essentially to the welfare and happiness of mankind. Each of these may be said to constitute a kind of era, which marks the progress of time in a very decided manner, forces upon the notice of even the most giddy and thoughtless, the recollection that another week, or month, or year, has passed by, and involves in this recollection the awful certainty, that the stream of time is flowing fast away, and must speedily be swallowed up in the ocean of eternity. With a very large portion of mankind, the smoothness with which time glides away resembles the travelling of an easy carriage : its progress would be often forgotten, were it not for certain occasional stoppages which remind them that it has been in motion, and that it is carrying them forward with a rapid, though insensible pace, " towards that bourne from whence no traveller returns."

There is no season which may more aptly be compared to one of these stages in the great journey of life, and which induces more serious reflection in a considerate mind, than that at which we have just arrived. The period when one year finishes, and another commences, forms an epoch in our lives, which is perhaps more strongly marked than any other. At this season, too, our minds are in an especial manner prepared for serious contemplation, by the recent commemoration of one of the most important events that the world has ever known—the birth of the Redeemer of mankind—an event, which should fill our minds with the most solemn awe, and our hearts with the most lively sensations of gratitude and devotion.

At this period, it is natural as well as profitable to look back on past events. When we recal to mind the road we have travelled, and the scenes we have witnessed, how chequered is the prospect which memory presents to our view! the sports of childhood, the hopes of youth, the opening prospects of manhood rise in review before us, with their accompanying train of fears, anxieties, and disappointments. It has, however, been justly remarked, that " we have many days of pleasure for one of pain, many hours of health for one of sickness;" and to a mind not jaundiced by prejudice, nor distempered by vice, the retrospect of life will afford a thousand recollections we shall fondly cherish, and ten thousand mercies which demand our warmest gratitude.

If the above remarks are found to hold good with mankind in general, *to us* they must apply with peculiar force and energy: for surely, Sir, few human creatures have more cause for serious contemplation, or for sincere and lively thankfulness than ourselves! Let us but look back for one year, and consider what our situation and prospects were. The greater part of us had just returned from a similar enterprise, vexed and mortified at the ill success which we had met with. Our own hopes, and those of our country, disappointed, nothing appeared left for us, but a long season of inactivity, and leisure to brood over the past!

How different is the prospect we have now before us! Selected once more for this interesting service—placed in a situation of credit and honour, which the sons of noblemen may reasonably envy, and which thousands of our own profession and rank would gladly fill—with the eyes of our country and of all Europe fixed upon us—how highly should we value these proud distinctions! If we further consider the extraordinary success which has attended our labours, what heart is there among us that does not beat high with exultation and hope? Could it have been predicted to us before we left England, that we should winter comfortably in a secure harbour of our own finding, near the 111th degree of longitude, who that is accustomed to the navigation of icy seas, would not have declared this to be success beyond his most sanguine expectations? And yet it is even so—we have succeeded in breaking the spell, which made the sea of Baffin a *bay*, have advanced near five hundred miles directly towards Behring's Strait, and found a secure port just when the season unexpectedly closed upon us, and obliged us to relinquish further operations.

Nor have we, in accomplishing this much of our enterprise, suffered privation or want of any kind. We have been abundantly supplied with all the necessaries, and many of the luxuries of life—we have most of us enjoyed our health—our ships have been preserved uninjured, under circumstances of frequent and unavoidable danger; and being furnished with resources which will enable us to renew the attempt with the same vigour as at first, we seem destined by Providence to decide a great geographical question, which, for centuries past, has been an object of curiosity to every nation in Europe.

Perhaps no expedition which England has

ever equipped, has been regarded with a more hearty feeling of national interest, than those in which we have been employed. Persons of every rank, and age, and sex, flocked to our ships—the philosopher approved a scheme whose object was the promotion of science—statesmen and prelates condescended to visit those, whose names might perhaps grace the page of future history—the merchant hoped that we might find a shorter way to China—the patriot, that we might add new lustre to Old England's glory—and, to crown all, the smile of beauty beamed upon us from every quarter, to inspire us with fresh ardour in the accomplishment of our glorious enterprise! The remembrance of these visits should long be cherished in our breasts: they were cordial and unequivocal expressions of regard from a warm-hearted and affectionate nation!

We cannot, perhaps, expect that this general interest should continue still to operate in the same degree as at first; for the public feeling is seldom very long fixed to one point—but how strongly would that interest be re-excited, could information of our present situation and prospects be at this time conveyed to England! A new field would be opened to speculation—the northern boundary of America would assume a more decided character upon the maps—the sanguine would be confirmed in their expectations, and even the most cautious sceptic would be forced to admit—not only the great probability of the *existence* of a north-west passage, but that there is some chance of its being at length actually effected.

But highly as it becomes us to appreciate the warm interest which the country at large has evinced for the success of our enterprise, there is another feeling, which, even in a still greater degree, must come home to the bosom of every one among us—I mean the anxious solicitude which must now be entertained by our relations and friends. Happy as we should undoubtedly be to remove some part of their anxiety, by making them acquainted with the comforts of our present situation; yet by a certain feeling inseparable from human nature, and no doubt implanted in our breasts for wise and benevolent purposes, there is, perhaps, nothing which produces a more exquisite degree of gratification than the certainty of our being the objects of that very solicitude to those we love. Whatever contradiction this may at first appear to involve, and whatever perverseness it may seem to argue in the constitution of our nature, yet it would be hard to call that selfishness, which leaves upon the most tender conscience no impression of wrong, and which is, in fact, the source of one of the purest and most refined pleasures of which we are capable.

At the season of Christmas, when it is customary for all the branches of a family to assemble around the same social fire-side, it is natural for them to think much of those who are wanting, to complete the circle. All expectation of our return this winter will now be at an end, and a severe conflict of contending emotions will succeed—the hope that our absence indicates success—the apprehension that some untoward accident has befallen us—at one moment, perhaps, exulting at the thoughts of our success, and firmly suppressing every wish but for our eventual benefit, they anticipate with proud and eager delight the time when we shall return to them with credit and honour, to reap the rewards of our labours—at another, imagination presents us to their view, suffering under privation or disease, and exposed to all the rigour of this inhospitable climate—then will nature break forth, in spite of every exertion—the tear of silent

I

anguish will be shed—the fervent prayer of pious devotion be offered to Heaven for our safety!

The considerations which I have now urged, and in which I have endeavoured to set forth some of the circumstances by which our situation is distinguished, should make us especially careful that our conduct be such as to justify the expectations which our country and our friends have formed of us. They have performed their part by placing us in our present station;—it remains for us to prove ourselves deserving of that station—not merely by the ardour which, as young men, we have all naturally felt at the beginning of a great and honourable enterprise—not by occasional sallies of zeal and exertion, which relapse into carelessness and inactivity as soon as the occasion ceases—but by a steady, uniform, and honest principle of duty, unmoved by circumstance, unshaken by difficulty, unaltered by time. We should reflect that our station can, in itself, confer no real dignity or honour: it is only the medium through which our good or bad conduct will be made the more conspicuous; it is the hinge on which our future hopes and prospects in the world must inevitably turn.

Above all—amidst the bustle of active life, and the discharge of our public duties, let us never forget what we owe to God and to our neighbour. Immured as we are together for a certain period, and secluded from the rest of the civilized world, it is no less our interest than our duty to keep a constant guard over our conduct towards each other. We should be particularly careful to restrain the natural irritability of temper, to which all are more or less subject; to check the risings of peevishness and ill-humour; to forgive others, as we ourselves hope to be forgiven. Let us ever be ready to assist each other in all the kindly offices which smooth the rugged path of life; and discarding all those petty animosities, those little passions, which serve but to disturb the tranquillity of society, and to disgrace us as Christians and as men, let us cordially unite with heart and hand in the great work we have undertaken.

By whatever distance we may be separated from our country and our friends; let us remember that we are ever mutually present with God! His all-seeing eye beholds us at one glance, his arm is ever stretched out to protect us—the mercy and beneficence of the Almighty are equally extended to us, whether we traverse the frozen regions of the north, or bask in the sunshine of our native plains.

I am, Sir,
Yours, &c.,
AMICUS.

For the WINTER CHRONICLE.

THOUGHTS ON NEW YEAR'S DAY, A. D. 1820.

THE moments of chasten'd delight are gone by,
  When we left our loved homes o'er new regions to rove,
When the firm manly grasp, and the soft female sigh,
  Mark'd the mingled sensations of friendship and love.

That season of pleasure has hurried away,
  When through far-stretching ice a safe passage we found *,
That led us again to the dark rolling sea,
  And the signal was seen " on for Lancaster's Sound †."

The joys that we felt when we pass'd by the shore,
  Where no footstep of man had e'er yet been imprest,
When rose in the distance no mountain-tops hoar,
  As the sun of the evening bright gilded the west ‡;
Full swiftly they fled—and that hour too is gone
  When we gain'd the meridian assign'd as a bound §,
To entitle our crews to their country's first boon,
  Hail'd by all as an omen the passage was found.

And past with our pleasures, are moments of pain;
  Of anxious suspense, and of eager alarm—
Environ'd by ice, skill and ardour were vain
  The swift moving mass of its force to disarm;
Tho' dash'd on the beach, and our boats torn away,
  No anchors could hold us, nor cable secure;
The dread and the peril expired with the day,
  When none but high Heaven could our safety ensure.

Involved with the ages existent before
  Is the year that has brought us thus far on our way,
And gratitude calls us, our God to adore
  For the oft-renew'd mercies its annals display;
The gloomy meridian of darkness is past,
  And ere long shall gay Spring and the herbage revive,
O'er the wide waste of ice shall re-echo the blast,
  And the firm prison'd ocean its fetters shall rive.

Now dawns the New Year! but what mind can expose
  The events that await us before it expires?
In the isles of the south to remember its close,
  Or in regions of frost mourn our frustrate desires!
Yet Hope points the track that our vessels shall force
  Till Pacific's wide ocean around us we view;
Bright Hope shall expand as we follow our course,
  And the dangers we meet but our courage renew.

* Our ships were the first that succeeded in effecting a passage to the westward, through the ice which occupies the middle of Baffin's Bay in the early part of the summer.

† Telegraphic signal made by the Hecla, after breaking through the first barrier of ice.

‡ The evening was beautifully clear when we sailed *over* the spot assigned to CROKER's MOUNTAINS.

§ The meridian of 110° west, which entitled us to the first reward of 5,000*l.*

The friends we have left, at this season of mirth
   Do their bosoms or pleasure or anguish sustain ?
Do they deem us yet safe in these wilds of the earth,
   Or whelm'd in the surges that whiten the main ?
No longer they now can expect our return,
   No longer they mark ev'ry change of the breeze ;
But the thought of despair fond affection will spurn,
   And confident rest on Almighty decrees !

With them we but share the proud hope of success,
   And look forward with joy to the days yet to come ;
When, the heart overflowing, warm tears shall express
   How sincere is the welcome that greets us at home ;
Be happiness theirs while we severed remain !—
   Be fortitude firm, and exertion, our own !
Till the shores of Old Albion once more we regain,
   Once more to enjoy every bliss we have known.

THE

NORTH GEORGIA GAZETTE,

AND

WINTER CHRONICLE.

Nº. XI—MONDAY, JANUARY 10, 1820.

To the EDITOR *of the* Winter Chronicle.

SIR,

SHELTERED under the indolent plea of inability, I have never taken any other part in our theatrical amusements than that of a spectator. I have, however, been a constant attendant, and witnessing the strenuous efforts made by each amateur, I have felt no small degree of concern at the loss of time, and the immensity of trouble, which these exertions occasion ; the time which is necessarily occupied in studying new, and sometimes long parts, and the trouble and expense, (if I may be allowed to apply the word to the sacrifice of sheets, curtains, and various other articles,) of preparing new dresses on every occasion, must be a very serious tax, particularly to those gentlemen who have other and more pleasing pursuits

to occupy the leisure which this season of inactivity affords.

Moreover, it is well known how very limited the theatrical library is, and, judging from the representation on Thursday evening, I am inclined to think, the small stock of pieces that contained humour suited to the audience, has been exhausted.

The good effects produced by the plays are too obvious to be questioned ; and I should be the first to lament their discontinuance, until our labours recommence ; but considering the very great amusement and gratification which the men have derived from the former representations, why, let me ask, might not some of them be repeated ? Far be it from me to impute the slightest blame either to the manager or committee, who are entitled, (especially the manager,) to our best and warmest thanks for the pains which they have taken; but is it not possible that in their zeal for the public welfare, they may overlook the best means of accomplishing the object in view?

If their aim is, as I believe, the amusement of the men, surely the most effectual way of obtaining this, would be to repeat those pieces from which they have already derived the greatest share; why not act again the amusing farce with which the theatre so successfully opened? Why should not Jack again enjoy the humours of Jerry Sneak? But, above all, why is not the *North West Passage* repeated? This piece, which cost so much in preparation, was got up so successfully, and which not only gave the most ecstatic delight to the men during representation, but afforded them in the recollection a fund of amusement even to this day— why, I say, should it be thrown by, as if it had wholly failed? Surely, Sir, this is an oversight that only needs to be pointed out to be remedied. Permit me then, through the medium of your valuable columns, to offer these remarks to the committee, which nothing but a strong conviction of their truth would have dictated; and at the same time to make the best apology I can to your readers, by assuring them that the general good of our community has been my first and only purpose in this communication.

I am, Mr. Editor, &c. &c. &c.,

A Looker-on.

To the Editor *of the* Winter Chronicle.

Sir—Understanding that it is in the contemplation of several gentlemen to establish a new weekly paper, for the purpose of affording greater scope to the exuberance of genius, which I am sure, from your well-known liberality of sentiment, will meet with your most cordial support, I am emboldened,

humble as my pretensions are, to solicit the public patronage, and offer myself as the Editor.

To discharge the duties of this office satisfactorily, it is not requisite that I should possess an extraordinary degree of intellect; for, unlike editors in general, who have to insert their own lucubrations to fill a vacant page, I am doubly assured by the very high opinion I entertain of the talents of its intended supporters, and by their own repeated professions of strenuously exerting them, that the only difficulty in my way will be the selection of such strokes of satire, or flashes of wit, as may best accord with the taste of the moment.

I am positive that nothing flat, low, or insipid, will ever be found on my files—a few touches beyond the sublimity of Milton; a style more easy and elegant than Addison; powers more splendid and versatile than Shakspeare's may occasionally be met with; but no paucity of materials, (except it be of paper,) to perpetuate the literary fame of the independent and highly-gifted youths, whose chosen servant I am anxious to become.

I think I can command every requisite for immediate publication; pens and ink I have no objection to furnish, and paper for the early numbers, provided they do not require more than three sheets each. One quill-driving (not printers') devil, I am prepared with, and a second is in training. The liberality of a friend has furnished me with an empty puncheon, in one of the heads of which I intend having a slit cut for the reception of contributions. These particulars are enumerated to demonstrate the very great interest I take in the cause, and I hope the reasons which have been adduced will be deemed sufficient to prove, that an editor for a work which promises to establish an era in the annals of literature may be found in one possessing only the feeble judgment, contracted mind, and circumscribed invention of,

Sir, your most obedient Servant,
HENRY HARMLESS.

To the EDITOR *of the* Winter Chronicle.

Mr. EDITOR—Will any of your correspondents assign a reason, or hazard a conjecture, why the freshening of the wind should be accompanied by a considerable rise in the temperature of the air; which we have found, I believe, invariably the case, from whatever direction the wind blows.

I am, Sir, *&c. &c. &c.,*
A CONSTANT READER.

THEATRICAL REPORT.

ON Thursday evening the officers of the Expedition performed the farce of *Bon Ton,* or *High Life above Stairs.* It happened unfortunately that the weather, which promised fair in the morning became inclement in the afternoon, and continued so much so during the performance, as materially to inconvenience the performers, and to lessen the gratification which the audience would otherwise have received from their exertions.

We are informed that the thermometer was at twelve degrees below zero on the stage, a degree of cold ill suited to the dresses of the fair sex especially.

Whilst on the subject of our theatrical entertainments, we beg leave to return our thanks to the contributor of the first article of the present number. We are persuaded that many of our readers will join with us, in the hope that its subject will not be deemed beneath the consideration of the committee of stage-management.

Theatre Royal, North Georgia.

MEN.

	Colonel Feignwell,	Mr. PARRY.	
Freeman, CAPTAIN SABINE.		Sir Philip Modelove,	Mr. GRIFFITHS.
Obadiah Prim,	Mr. WAKEHAM.	Tradelove,	Mr. HOPPNER.
Periwinkle,	Mr. NIAS.	Sackbut,	Mr. BUSHNAN.
Simon Pure,	Mr. BEVERLEY.	Amminadab,	Mr. HALSE.

WOMEN.

Mrs. Prim,	Mr. HOOPER.	Ann Lovely,	Mr. ROSS.

SONGS as usual will be interspersed.

Doors to be opened at Half-past Six, and the Performance to commence at Seven o'Clock.

---

* You 're the characters cast, and now guess at the play ;
But wait! I'll endeavour to shew you the way ;
The Play that 's to steal a dull hour of your life,
By the Author was named—*A Bold Stroke for a Wife.*
The day that 's appointed is next Wednesday week,
Should it not be too cold for the Actors to speak.

The Committee of the Theatre request the Editor will give publicity to their disavowal of any participation in Snip Quill-drive's Letter, which appeared in the 9th Number of the *Winter Chronicle.*

---

* In writing the fair copy of this Number for circulation on board, the date and title of the play were accidentally forgotten, when these lines were subjoined to supply the omission.

The following communication reached us on Friday night, but just in time to save the press. On reading it, we perceived that the writer is suffering under a grievance, which, so far as we understand him, makes him urgent for the immediate insertion of his letter. We have, therefore, been induced to wave the *consideration* which it is our custom to give to the articles with which we fill our columns, and have submitted his letter, without delay, to our readers.

To the Editor *of the* Winter Chronicle.

I am rather surprised, Mr. Editor, since I believe the original intention of the *Winter Chronicle* was exceedingly foreign to what appears, by degrees, to have crept into it, and which is far on the climax to decided personality; I mean the various attacks made on the several members of our community. Mine, Mr. Editor, is a case in which a pair of calves were declared to have strayed from their owner's, No. 1, Bell-lane, next door to the Club-room. Now, as I am confident you are a man who values a respectable reputation in an infinitely higher degree than the advantages derived from your Weekly Numbers, I consider it my duty to warn you against a person who, at this time, I am aware, constitutes a small part of the little society who contribute to its weekly existence; for I understand, and that from the most respectable authority, that the said person is in the habit of, what I suppose he would call revising, but from the accounts I have of the matter, absolutely altering and re-modelling it, according to his own fancy. Since this is the case, I am strongly led to imagine that the advertisement alluded to was intended for a neighbour of mine, residing in Ordnance-square, next door to Apothecaries' Hall, whose calves, I know

strayed some time ago, and I hear have now entirely left him : not mine, Mr. Editor ; on the contrary, mine indeed, are at this time in an exceedingly forward state. I am naturally fond of the picturesque, and therefore have them in front of my premises. I take as much delight in them as I do in my very self, and shall for ever have them before me. This, Mr. Editor, is not the whole of my complaint. I was the other day absolutely insulted to my face ! ! As I was sitting at my table, studying in happy quiet, who should pop in but one of your devils : the impudent fellow, regardless of my age and infirmities, commenced his insinuations, and by degrees told me I was the identical little man alluded to in your gazette. I have, Mr. Editor, patronised it from its commencement, and, as my residence in some degree excommunicates me from society, no part of it fails to excite my strictest scrutiny. But I shall proceed with my grievance, he explained to me, as I said before, that " I was the little man stated to have risen from the band-box, and that I also, one day or the other, would be subject to a hen-pecking."—It would have been as well for the scribbler had he kept this part of his article in his inkstand—for here I have him—I have often expressed my intention never to marry ; and suppose I should ? I well remember the opinion of a friend of mine, who was kind enough to sympathize and condole with me, on a similar occasion ; and as he is a man who has lived longer, and I am sure, knows more of the world than I do, I consider his first-rate authority. He said—" That little men were usually marked with extraordinary talents—that they were so polite, so kind, so every thing a lady could wish ;" and, therefore, I am almost confident they are subject to less purgatory than persons of a contrary description. And suppose the conclusion here drawn to be perfect, I may rely, Mr. Editor, on leading a most quiet and peaceable life, were I to venture to-morrow to the matrimonial shrine. Trusting you will be convinced of the perfect fiction of the one case, and in some degree, if not altogether, coinciding with my hypothesis in the other, which appears to me to be tolerably well founded, I conclude, trusting you will in future, for the sake of your reputation, examine your paper immediately previous to its appearance in public, that such alterations which your printers may have taken upon them to make, may, by your timely scrutiny, resume their originality, and thereby rescue your chronicle from impending defamation, which will await it, if this my prescription be not enforced.

I am, Mr. Editor,

Your sincere well-wisher,

N. C.

P. S. You will pardon the shocking state, Mr. Editor, in which I put this to your hand, not being Friday night; and strongly at this moment provoked, I send this rough as it is, in order if any case relative to N°. 1, Bell-lane, be intended for insertion in your next Number, you may have an opportunity of preventing it.

Advertisements, &c.

A NEW WEEKLY PAPER!

On SATURDAY, the FIRST DAY of APRIL, 1820, Will be published the First Number of a new Weekly Paper, to be called,

THE NON-CONTRIBUTOR'S POST;

OR,

OPPOSITION JOURNAL.

PROSPECTUS.

As the design of this paper is solely to act in opposition to the *Winter Chronicle*, Sir Stephen Stingall, who has undertaken to be the editor, will consider himself responsible that no article whatever shall be omitted, which to his knowledge contains an attack upon any individual of the chroniclers, reserving to himself, however, the discretionary power of adding to or altering any contributions, which may appear to him to admit of more pointed satire, or on any other similar account, and of either briefly assigning his reasons, or otherwise, as he may think proper.

Original contributions on this subject, consistent with the plan of the Paper, will be acceptable. The Editor begs it, however, to be distinctly understood, that he is wholly independent of the gentlemen of the Expedition for its support, he having laid in, on his own account, a sufficient stock of the necessary ingredients to answer all the purposes of the N. C. P. Orders and communications, if post-paid, will meet with immediate attention, on being addressed to the Editor at the O. P. library, Fleet-market, where may be obtained all the periodical pamphlets of the day.

.*. Stationary supplied.
Book-binding in all its branches.

THE
NORTH GEORGIA GAZETTE,

PER·FRETA·HACTENUS·NEGATA·

AND
WINTER CHRONICLE.

Nº. XII—MONDAY, JANUARY 17, 1820.

To the EDITOR *of the* Winter Chronicle.

SIR,

It is not to be wondered at, that our having observed, on Wednesday last, the greatest degree of natural cold ever before recorded*, should have excited a considerable interest in the minds of your correspondents; for, independently of its being an interesting fact in the history of our voyage, it seems to have served the useful purpose of relieving us from that dull monotony, with which, for some weeks past, one day has succeeded another. Nor can any thing be more natural, and I may justly add, more praiseworthy, than the eagerness with which it has been debated at our tables, whether the thermometer stood at 50½, or 50¾, that is, whether we beat the rest of the world by half, or by three quarters of a degree! I have even heard it asserted by one gentleman, who seems determined to hand our names down to posterity with all the honour which extreme frost can confer, that the thermometer actually and fairly, and without any fudging, or wincing of an eye, stood at −51 for upwards of half an hour! In order to decide the matter, I beg to make your readers acquainted with the result of some very careful and minute observations made by myself on the only two thermometers used on that eventful day. They

---

* Fifty degrees and a half below Zero; this, however, is not the greatest degree of natural cold on record;—57 is said to have been observed by Mr. Von Elterlein, at Vytegra in the Russian dominions, on the 5th of January 1780. ED.

were made with one of Dollond's eight feet achromatic telescopes, of great magnifying power, with a micrometer-scale applied to it by myself in a very ingenious manner, by which I found thermometer N°. 1 to intimate $-50°.615$, and N°. 2 $-50°.845$. The mean of these, *viz.*, $50°.730$ may, I think, be fairly stated as the actual degree of cold to be registered. I trust, Sir, that the care with which these observations were conducted, the excellence of the instruments employed, and my well-known skill in these matters, will be sufficient to set this most interesting and important question at rest for ever; and that your readers will be satisfied that they have as yet *out-shivered* the rest of the habitable globe only by 730 thousandth parts of a single degree of Fahrenheit's scale.

I am, Mr. Editor,

Your modest, humble Servant,

SIMON SET-RIGHT.

P. S. Being desirous to add all in my power to our frigorific fame, it is my intention to renew my observations whenever the thermometer again falls below par, and I doubt not I shall be able by means of some improvements now in hand, to screw out another quarter of a degree of cold, for the benefit of our meteorological journals.

Since writing the above, I have re-examined my instruments, and think I have discovered an index-error of two thousandth parts nearly. I cannot refuse myself the gratification of assuring your readers that this error is additive, and therefore all in our favour.

––––––

Before we give publicity to the subsequent letters, occasioned by an article which we inserted in our last Number bearing the signature of N. C., we beg to offer a few remarks to the consideration of our correspondents and of our readers, but especially of the former.

From the commencement of our undertaking we have been aware of the delicate ground on which we suffered ourselves to be placed, in admitting articles containing personal allusions, however inoffensive. We were induced, however, to take upon ourselves this responsibility, requiring a more than ordinary caution, by the following considerations; first, the difficulty which our Correspondents represented, of finding other subjects productive of equal amusement, with which to fill our columns;—second, from our experience of the care so assiduously maintained on the one side, to keep strictly within the bounds of playful and harmless raillery, and of the thorough good-humour with which it was met on the other:—third, from witnessing the entertainment which our readers received from these communications; and, finally, perhaps, from feeling that we had it in our power to put a period to them, whenever they should approach the limits which had been hitherto respected. We were not, indeed, without a hope, that in the course of time, such subjects would give place to others of more intrinsic merit, and useful as well as entertaining. This consideration augmented the gratification with which we received the excellent letter which forms the greater part of our tenth Number; and we are happy in believing, that were this letter viewed in no other light than as an experiment, to ascertain how far matters of useful, and even of serious, tendency, would be appreciated by the readers of the *Winter Chronicle* at their just value, the result was most highly satisfactory and encouraging.

We should have preferred awaiting the ordinary progress of this change in the subjects chosen by our contributors, without endeavouring to hasten it by any remarks of our own, had we not been constrained to the present notice by the letter of N. C. above-mentioned ; not merely in consequence of his advice, for which we return him our acknowledgments, but because he has himself indulged, even beyond his predecessors, in the practice which it was his especial object to caution us against.

We have availed ourselves of the occasion, to express thus much of our sentiments, persuaded that our correspondents will ever remember with ourselves, that it is of far more importance to avoid giving pain, than to amuse, and that self-love will frequently point a shaft, which is designed to be, and is in itself, entirely harmless.

To the EDITOR *of the* Winter Chronicle.

MR. EDITOR—I have ever considered cheerfulness as a duty we owe to society ; and regarding your papers as a means of promoting good humour among us, I have always felt disposed to receive entertainment from the lively sallies of wit which have occasionally filled its columns, notwithstanding they have sometimes approached that " climax of decided personality," which N. C. complains of, and towards which he certainly advances some few steps beyond any of his competitors.

Nor should I now, Mr. Editor, feel any disposition to complain of the liberty taken with my person, had your Correspondent clothed the words, which he has thought proper to put into my mouth, in good honest English dress ; but when, on Monday morning last, I heard read from your columns, a letter, purporting to come from my residence, No. 1, Bell-lane, I own that I felt a strong desire to detect the author. After the butch-

ery that had been committed, I had no hopes of seeing the strayed *calves,* but I thought it possible a mangled limb might be detected ; and on looking minutely around the table, I am sure I espied a solitary head served up without the usual garniture of brains : but this was not sufficient evidence, and I had recourse to a second reading of the letter ; but the difficulty of comprehending it gave me little hopes of success. I fancied, however, that in the writer's extreme fondness for the " picturesque," and his determination to have calves in the front of his premises, instead of the usual ornaments of Mercury's, Hercules's, &c. &c., I could discover a strong smell of the citizen ; and I was the more inclined to this opinion, when I found the quotation of " so kind, so polite," &c.; because this is well known to be the language of the city only, and used by the fair admirers of the Major Sturgeons of the day.

But all this, Mr. Editor, amounts only to suspicion ; and as I am fond of plain-dealing, I resolved to request you to give publicity to my disavowal of the letter written in my name, and to my desire that the gentleman, whoever he may be, will not again choose me for the father of his wit.

I am, Mr. Editor,
Your humble Servant,
JOSEPHUS NOT-FAR-OFF.

To the EDITOR *of the* Winter Chronicle.

SIR—I remember having once read, in *Gulliver's Travels,* of a machine, the motion of which formed letters into words, and words into sentences ; and it is to a similar mechanical source that I ascribe the letter of N. C. in your last number.

It appears, however, to be the effort of a novice in the management of the book-making apparatus; for had the instrument usually produced such effects, not even the sages of Laputa had tolerated its use. I would advise your Correspondent to try another turn, and if this fails another yet; but should he still find himself unsuccessful, he may try what it will avail to write the sentences produced in two columns, when, perhaps, the cross-readings may be a nearer approximation to sense. Beginners are ever in a hurry for the completion of their scheme, and I think it probable such a feeling may have induced the artist, instead of waiting for the production of syllables from their elements, (letters,) to throw in ready-made words of so hard a nature, as to cause the injury of the mechanism. But I may be wrong in my conclusion ; and, therefore, confessing my own total inability to discover the secret, request that you will inform me what meaning, if there be any at all, attaches to the paper in question.

I remain, Sir,

Your constant reader,

JOHN SLENDER-BRAIN.

To the EDITOR of the Winter Chronicle.

MR. EDITOR.—The perusal of an article in your last week's Number, has strangely puzzled me: that much labour had been expended in its composition was sufficiently obvious; but after repeated readings, or attempts to read it through, I had well nigh despaired of discovering the object of so much pains; when a surmise suggested itself to me, which, amongst the many conjectures which I have heard in the course of the week, is the only one that supplies any satisfactory method of accounting for it.

It is well known, Mr. Editor, that the Non-contributors to your columns, anxious to prove that inability has not kept them silent, have been of late making a strong canvass to establish an opposition paper. Now, as in all warfare, stratagems are resorted to, may it not be as important to weaken an enemy's position as to strengthen one's own? Consider then this extraordinary letter, as the joint production of the junto of opposition, written with the insidious design of raising a laugh at the expense of the paper which should insert it; wearing the semblance of grievance and complaint, to secure a reception which it might not otherwise have found; intended, moreover, perhaps, as a subject for the first essay of opposition-criticism on the 1st of April; and it cannot fail to strike you as so well adapted for the purpose, as to give considerable probability to my surmise.

It may then be deemed a fair sample of the talent and ingenuity, perverted, perhaps, in this one instance, with which you will have to contend; exerted here most successfully in producing a laboured composition which shall appear at first sight perfectly *natural*.

Should the master-hand that directs this knot of oppositionists possess, in an equal degree, the skill of producing the reverse effect to the present; should he, in other words, be able to extract a meaning, and re-model in an intelligible form, such a heterogeneous composition as the letter of N. C., I fear his success against you will be inevitable.

My purpose, Mr. Editor, has been to put you on your guard against attempts of this kind in future; perhaps, also, in ascribing the letter of N. C. to the quarter I have pointed out, you may partake of the advantage which I have found, in being able to join heartily in the frequent laughs which it has occasioned, unembarrassed by the fear that the mirth of some one unfortunate wight of the laughers around me was assumed, to shield him from a quiz which he had brought on himself.

   I am, Mr. Editor,
    Your humble Servant,
     SMELL-RAT SMOKE'EM.

OBITUARY.

On Monday, the 9th instant, between the hours of six and eight in the morning, died, in the prime of life, John Gull *, a youth of very promising talents, and extraordinary endowments. He was descended from an ancient and respectable family in the north, and was on his travels to see the world, accompanied by his twin-sister, when he was suddenly snatched away, leaving her to deplore his irreparable loss. It is supposed that had he lived to reach England, he would have obtained one of the first situations vacant in the British Museum.

Advertisements.

TWO GUINEAS REWARD.

LOST, within the last month, a LINDLEY MURRAY's GRAMMAR and BROWN's FOLIO DICTIONARY. The owner having much occasion for them, and labouring under serious inconvenience from their loss, is induced to offer the above reward to any person or persons, who may have found, and will return the same to his [residence, Rudder-Head-House, near After-Hold, within the ensuing week.

Early in May will be published, in One Volume Octavo, neatly bound in Calf,

CLAVIS CHRONICLARIA ;

OR,

A KEY TO THE WINTER CHRONICLE,

Containing a full and [correct account of the Author of each article in that Paper, with fac-similes of several of the hand-writings.

BY PETER PRY-ABOUT.

This Work is also designed to contain criticisms on many of the learned communications, both in prose and verse, which are found in the columns of the Gazette, with copious annotations, elucidations, and illustrations, of several obscure, and apparently unintelligible, passages. The Author has spared neither time nor labour to merit the public patronage and encouragement ; and will feel extremely obliged by any communications which may assist in rendering his work more complete. He will be particularly thankful for all hints which may tend to elucidate any part of N. C.'s letter, in the Eleventh Number of the Chronicle, as the Author freely confesses himself at a loss either to discover the writer, to unravel the mysterious intricacies of his plot, or even in some parts to trace the language to that of any known nation, in ancient or modern times.

---

* One of a pair of glaucous gulls, which had been taken from a nest on one of the North Georgian Islands in the summer, and brought up on board ; when full grown they shewed no disposition to quit the ship.

THE
NORTH GEORGIA GAZETTE,

PER·FRETA·HACTENUS·NEGATA·

AND
WINTER CHRONICLE.

Nº. XIII—MONDAY, JANUARY 24, 1820.

To the Editor *of the* Winter Chronicle.

Mr. Editor,

I will not endeavour to conceal from you or your readers, the mortification I felt at hearing your last week's paper read at the breakfast-table on Monday morning. You must indeed confess, that a paper almost exclusively devoted to lampoons upon one unfortunate wight, was sufficient to appal an author much more accustomed than myself to the free and unrestrained attacks of public criticisms. But, as soon as the roar of merriment, which the contents of your columns had raised at my expense, had subsided, and I had leisure only to reflect on what had passed, I felt convinced that however severe a roasting your correspondents had thought proper to give me, I had certainly brought it upon my own

shoulders, and that any attack which might be made on my letter was only a return in kind, of which I had no right to complain. It has always been my wish to contribute my mite to the support of your paper, because I consider it the duty of every member of a community to do his best to promote the public welfare. And, that your paper tends to promote that object, no sensible man will, of course, doubt. But something or other, Mr. Editor, has always come in the way, to prevent my putting my intention in execution, till Old Nick in an evil hour, persuaded me to drop into your box the letter of the unfortunate N. C., which letter, as all your readers know, might as well, to use my own expression, have been " kept in my ink-stand." Having heard it hinted, however, by several persons whose good taste and judgment I highly respect, that the subject of my letter and not its style was the real occasion of the general attack made upon it, I am induced to flatter myself that it was not quite so badly written as some of your witty and facetious friends pretended; and, I have even some hopes that by giving my compositions another turn in the machine, as recommended by John Slenderbrain, I may perhaps produce something more worthy a place in one of your future Numbers. Be this as it may, I have derived great satisfaction from the perfect good humour with which every shaft has been pointed against my first literary effort, and I beg to assure you, that no other feeling exists on my part towards the individual who has justly taxed me with " choosing him for the father of my wit," or towards any of those who, in espousing the cause of my friend Josephus Not-far-off, have handled poor N. C. thus severely.

Before I conclude my letter, I must notice the mistake into which the Non-contributors to your paper have fallen, in supposing my initials to have a reference to them, of all people under the sun! a mistake which has subjected me for this week past to a torrent of the most affectionate sympathy from some members of this now slender tribe. Now, Sir, I do think it rather hard, that I cannot be allowed to select any two letters from the alphabet for my anonymous signature, without having a little word tacked on to the first, and a confounded long one to the second, by any of those tender, sympathetic friends of mine who choose to try this method of enlisting me under their standard! As you are a military man, Mr. Editor, you must surely be aware that this is a most unwarrantable manner of making a man *take the shilling*.

As I am anxious to make known these my candid and undisguised sentiments without delay, I beg you will insert them, if you have room, in your next week's paper; both as a proof that I can take a joke as well as give one, and, as an earnest of the sincerity with which I remain, Mr. Editor,

Your friend and well-wisher,

N. C., *i. e.*, No Churl.

To the Editor of the Winter Chronicle.

Mr. Editor—I was agreeably surprised on reading in your last Number, the candid manner in which you suggested to your correspondents, the subjects you would prefer for the pages of the *Winter Chronicle*; I say, *agreeably surprised*, because I had been confidently assured your sentiments were widely different, and that " men of scientific knowledge were withheld from writing, because it was understood that nothing but the trifling nonsense that had lately appeared would be acceptable to the editor."

As I have a great regard for your paper, Mr. Editor, you will readily believe the satisfaction I felt on discovering the whole of this to be without foundation, and this satisfaction was considerably increased by the hope that another piece of scandal which had reached my ears might be equally untrue. This is no less a charge than that the original communications of your correspondents are altered, at the caprice, not of yourself indeed, but of those employed under your direction! When I first heard this, Mr. Editor, I could not help exclaiming it was impossible; but my informant assured me it was true. " Nay," says he, " the Editor has himself declared that he has no longer any control over the paper, and that his devils, in spite of all he can say, take upon themselves to alter the articles in such a manner, that when he again sees them in his columns, he is scarcely able to recognise them."

Now, Mr. Editor, if this be true, I have done; your paper must fall to the round;

and if it be not true, it is imperative upon you to contradict it, and, as a " word to the wise" is sufficient, I shall only add, that I am

Your sincere well-wisher,

VERITAS.

———————

We have not been able wholly to make up our minds whether we should consider the letter of " Veritas" as a squib ; or, in a more serious light, and according to its ostensible purport. Were we to judge by the contents alone, we should incline to the first opinion ; and as such should scarcely deem it worthy of insertion; but its style and signature wear the appearance at least of one who is no jester.

As we are always ready to give a reasonable explanation to those who ask it in a reasonable manner, we purpose a reply ; and we devote the necessary space with the less reluctance, because we have not often intruded ourselves on the attention of our readers, preferring at all times that they should be amused by our correspondents rather than by ourselves.

We notice, first, Veritas's principal alarm, that " original communications are altered at the caprice, not of the Editor indeed, but of those under his direction." Veritas professes to disbelieve " this piece of scandal," as he terms it; we shall, nevertheless, consider him in our reply as the person who made the observation, leaving it to the individual who really did so, if such one there was, to substitute his own name for that of Veritas, and he will find his answer.

Veritas must either be a contributor, or a non-contributor ; if the first, then has he not dealt fairly with us, since truth should have obliged him to acknowledge, that whatever others might say they had experienced, his papers had never been so improperly treated ; if, on the contrary, the ob-

jector be a non-contributor ; if, when others are employing their time, and using their best exertions for the public amusement, he has withheld, under the plea of inability or any other which he may wish to substitute in preference, the attempt to assist in promoting a public good, we should conceive that the matter of his objection is no concern of his ; that even if it had a foundation, it would be wholly between the writers and the Editor ; that those who do not write, certainly can have no title to find fault.

But a moment's thought might have satisfied Veritas, that if original communications had been so abused, we should have heard long since an outcry from the writers themselves. No person would see his composition altered without appealing to the Editor, who well knows, that if redress were refused, he would soon find that individual case, (and not the vague surmise that such things may be) the subject of general remark.

The Editor pays but a small portion of the acknowledgments due from the public to the gentlemen, facetiously termed by Veritas the " Editor's Devils," who have so kindly devoted a large portion of their weekly time to the task of transcribing the paper for their companions' perusal, when he takes the occasion to remark, that such is their habitual accuracy, that scarcely a single instance has come to his knowledge of even an accidental mistake having occurred in copying from the original documents; and these are sometimes not a little difficult to decipher. Verbal alterations are occasionally made by the Editor himself, though very sparingly ; for, he considers himself in no way responsible for the style, any more than for the arguments, sentiments, or consistency of the articles which pass through his hands, beyond his original engagement, to insert nothing which he thinks will give offence. Except such verbal alterations, none have been made, but with the knowledge and consent of the contributors themselves; and for such and for every alteration, whether accidental or otherwise, the Editor has been always aware of his responsibility to the authors, but to them alone; and as he has been careful heretofore, so he will continue to maintain his responsibility, and to be able to return an answer whenever he may see it expedient to do so.

We proceed to notice the other matter which Veritas has heard alleged against us, viz., " that men of scientific knowledge are withheld from writing, because it has been understood that nothing but the trifling nonsense which had lately appeared would be acceptable to the Editor." Veritas must pardon us if we hesitate to consider this otherwise than as a jest; as such, some one may have said it, but surely no one in earnest; for a moment's reflection would have reminded him, that our prospectus invited communications from writers of various descriptions, the philosopher amongst others; and that, in our first Number we took occasion to make known expressly, our desire to promote objects of scientific inquiry generally; we have also subsequently inserted letters at different times, requesting information on particular points of science; it is true these letters are unanswered, but we have not heard that any complaint has been made of answers having been sent, and not admitted. We can therefore very confidently affirm, that if " men of scientific knowledge" have been indeed " withheld from writing," alas! alas! some other cause must be sought to account for this backwardness on the part of these scientific gentlemen, than the fear lest their contributions should not be acceptable to the Editor. The fact is so obviously on the other side, that we scarcely suppose any

person could seriously commit himself in so gross an error as that which the words quoted by Veritas convey.

But we would address a few words to any person who is disposed to cavil at the *Winter Chronicle*, on the score of deficiency; who finds fault because such and such subjects do not occupy so much of its columns as he thinks they might with advantage. We would ask such a person, whether he has endeavoured to remedy the fault by sending an article himself on such subjects? and whether it has been refused admittance? If not we would ask him, does he know that any other person has tried and been unsuccessful? If he cannot answer these questions in the affirmative, he is manifestly without ground of complaint against the Editor, or the paper; and, if he is still disposed to censure, we recommend him to count up the number of officers in both ships, when he will know precisely how much of his censure falls to his own share, as well as be able to distribute to his friends around him, the exact amount of their proportions.

THEATRICAL REPORT.

On Wednesday evening was performed the Comedy of *A Bold Stroke for a Wife*; it gave us the most sincere pleasure to perceive, that the audience appeared to derive from this performance even greater amusement and delight than from any of the preceding entertainments. We are, indeed, of opinion that none of them have been kept up with more spirit and success throughout, than the present; and this will be considered as no mean praise by those who have been accustomed to private theatres, and who are aware of the difficulty with which a five-act play is usually supported by amateur performers.

The thermometer in the air was at 26° below zero; but such were the improvements made in the warming of the theatre, that the snow upon the roof was thawing within; a degree of warmth that contributed much to the comfort of the spectators and performers. We shall only repeat our conviction of the extreme usefulness of our theatrical entertainments, and cannot better express our good wishes than by a hope, that they may continue to be conducted in the same masterly manner which has hitherto ensured their success.

Theatre Royal, North Georgia.

On Wednesday, February 2, 1820, will be performed, for the second time this Season, the Farce of

MISS IN HER TEENS.

After which, the new Musical Entertainment of

THE NORTH-WEST PASSAGE;

OR,

THE VOYAGE FINISHED.

HYPERBOREAN BONNETS.

Miss Betty Scraggles begs leave to solicit the patronage of her country-women, in favour of the above elegant and tasteful article, to the improvement of which she has exclusively devoted her time since the commencement of winter; and is now extremely happy in being enabled to offer to the ladies, in this season of carol and hilarity, this *sine qua non* of the millinery world.

Miss Scraggles also flatters herself with the approbation of her patriotic country-women, for breaking the trammels of Parisian fashions, so long and unworthily borne.

Specimens of the above incomparable!! may be viewed by the fashionable dashers of the west end, at her bazaar, No. 2, Capstan-square; and for the accommodation of the fair citizens, at the manufactory, No. 10, Cheese-market, Pump-lane, City-road.

For the WINTER CHRONICLE.

Wild scenes of winter! what can ye disclose
To feast the sight or give the eye repose?
Can frozen grandeur, snows, or solid floods
Compete with Britain's fields, or waving woods?
Stern awe and horror ye may well inspire,
But not one pleasing thought, one fond desire.
No lover wand'ring thro' the leafy shade
In blissful converse with his charming maid,

Breathes in her ear the ardent vow of truth,
While she delighted hears the favour'd youth.
No warbling bird attunes the evening lay,
If o'er yon rugged hills we chance to stray;
No distant light proclaims the social dome,
No loved relations wait us at our home.
What pleasures then, from scenes so dear apart,
Have power with us to soothe the swelling heart?
What shall we deem the source of happiness
When Nature wears no more her lovely dress?
While, exiled from society, we roam
Where tempests roar, and sparkling surges foam?

   The mind, unsway'd by circumstance or time,
Confesses still its origin sublime;
Not lavish Nature, or the charms of Art,
Contentment or repose can e'er impart,
If sense of error wound the feeling breast,
By conscience unrelenting deep imprest.
True happiness in virtue must be sought,
Ensur'd at once, performing what we ought;
To others doing what we would receive;
The grief too poignant seeking to relieve,
To heal the wound that sorrow's shaft has made
With point more anguish'd than the reeking blade.
Each passion's sway restraining from excess,
And making thus our daily errors less;
Led by His word, who made and still sustains
This pendant orb, and o'er Creation reigns.
   Roll on, ye wintry hours! no real woe
Can all your stormy horrors yet bestow;
A transient gloom ye may awhile impose,
Like yonder cloud before the moon-beam rose;
But when the lamp of life shall feebly shine,
When youth's and manhood's fires alike decline:
And when the last loud trump shall bid us soar
To hear our doom, when " time shall be no more,"
The soul relying on the Saviour's power,
Shall stand undaunted in that awful hour.—
His will on earth perform'd—our God shall bless
And clothe the sinner with his righteousness !

                                                     C.

NOTICE TO CORRESPONDENTS.

The Editor wishes that a practice, which has prevailed of late, among some of his Correspondents, of personally delivering their contributions, may be discontinued. The box is always to be found on the Gun-room sky-light.

THE
NORTH GEORGIA GAZETTE,

PER · FRETA · HACTENUS · NE GATA.

AND
WINTER CHRONICLE.

N°. XIV—MONDAY, JANUARY 31, 1820.

To the EDITOR *of the* Winter Chronicle.

SIR—I cannot refrain from expressing to you my feelings, on hearing the keen, yet good-humoured, raillery, with which, in your last Number, you handled the subjects contained in the letter of Veritas. Methought every fresh sentence added fresh *goût* to the tea I was sipping, and I do not know when I have so much relished my bread and butter as on Monday morning last. You must know that I have been a constant, though perhaps unknown, admirer of your Paper, and have laboured through many dull lines in some of your columns, for the sake of the wit and ingenuity contained in others; and still more so for the general tendency of your plan. I have even scribbled hard to copy your Papers ; and mean, when we get home, to have the King's arms nicely printed at the head of each ; and if you will consent to sit for your picture, I have no objection to make you the frontispiece to the handsome little volume they will compose.

But your remarks upon Veritas's letter I mean to have neatly bordered with gold leaf, and surmounted with a long six-pounder on one side, and a Congreve's rocket on the other ; as emblems at the same time of your military profession, and of the skill with which you can *fire a shot* when occasion re-requires.

Before the appearance of your last Number, Mr. Editor, you had been very long silent, or, at best, had but mumbled out, now and then, a formal demi-official remark or two, or a theatrical puff, at proper intervals, as in editorial duty bound ; the consequence was, that some of your readers began to forget that you were not in the receipt of more than a thousand a-year by your labours! They apparently forgot, till you properly reminded them of it, that you cared not a straw whether they were pleased by the subjects chosen by your Correspondents or not; that you were one, among many other gentlemen, whose amusement you were endeavouring to promote, at the expense of a considerable portion of time and attention; which, as far as regarded yourself alone, might always be better employed; and that it was only just, that those who did not write should not be amused by those who did.

One thing, however, is evident, that the number of your Correspondents is weekly increasing; and that your Paper never stood on such firm footing as at present. The N. C.'s!—but alas, the very name is now almost extinct; and serves but to remind one of that beautiful and expressive idea of the Arabian MSS., which may thus be paraphrased—" I looked into the Editor's box, and cried ' the Non-Contributors where are they?' and Echo answered—' Where are they?'"

I am, Mr. Editor,
Your constant reader,
PETER PLAINWAY.

To the EDITOR *of the* Winter Chronicle.

MR. EDITOR—You made a fine palaver in your last paper about the accuracy of your devils: but this is to inform you, that even in my own communications, which are not numerous, I have discovered no less than seven *errata*, consisting of three DASHES altogether overlooked, one comma and two semicolons omitted; and once you and your devils, with a plague to you, made me come to a *full stop* when I had no such

meaning. You must know very well that there is often more latent sense concealed under a single mysterious *dash*,—or a well-applied note of admiration! than in all the rest of a letter put together; and, as an instance of the serious mistakes which have occurred for want of attention to correct punctuation, permit me to relate the following story: The day after a sailor went to sea, his wife called upon the parson, to desire the prayers of the parish for his safety; the clergyman consented, and wrote his memorandum accordingly as follows: " A man going to sea, his wife desires the prayers of the congregation:" but having unfortunately put the comma in the wrong place, he read it from the pulpit thus: " A man going to see his wife, desires the prayers of the congregation."

Now, Sir, it is, I suppose, by some such accident as this, that one or two of my best productions have been made absolute nonsense, when read at the breakfast-table; and, as I am sure you must commiserate the case of an unfortunate author, who is obliged to hear his productions thus tattered and torn; I trust you will take this hint as it is intended, and make your devils mind their p's and q's in future.

I remain, Mr. Editor,
Your well-wisher,
STEPHEN STOP-WELL.

HOSTILITIES IN THE NORTH.

GENERAL FROST continues to prosecute the siege of Fort Nature with every demonstration of vigour. The approaches have been pushed to the *foot* of the Glacis and some *horn-works* which covered it destroyed, but the defences of the *body* of the place are yet so numerous, that it is considered impossible to effect a breach, and the unremitting vigilance of the garrison precludes all hope of starving them; but various sallies have taken place, and many of the defenders have *fallen;* on the other hand, masses of the general's troops are almost daily captured, and those who escape the steel are given over to the *flames* *.

The *Army of Observation* †, has been a particular object of attack, but the only advantages which have as yet resulted, are the burning of one or two of the *bridges of communication,* whose defence had not been properly attended to. The general's opponents are, however, not idle, and his posts are incessantly annoyed by *red hot shot* ‡. Skirmishes happen every day, and frequent enterprises are attempted by the besiegers, but they are generally defeated with *loss,* although it is said that affairs have occurred, in which they have actually *surprised* their foes *in bed.*

Stratagem forms, apparently, a favourite part of the general's system, as a relation of his, with several adherents, were lately found concealed in the water-casks, and at present remain in " durance vile."

On a recent occasion, this officer is reported to have displayed a *degree of coolness* never before witnessed, which had the effect of imparting *surprising firmness* to his troops. It is truly remarkable, that though these troops await the charge perfectly immoveable, they *drop off* with great celerity when exposed to a *lively fire.* The general's forces are expected to be entirely broken early in the summer, and preparations are making for a vigorous pursuit; of the entire success of which the most sanguine hopes are entertained. PHILO-CALORIC.

A *Baker* § belonging to one of his Majesty's ships, who has long groaned under the tyranny of the *Boatswain* §, having by a hurt in his leg, become incapacitated for active duty, solicits the subscription of the charitable and humane, with a view to forming an establishment of his own; and being no *Pincher* §, hopes to ensure the favour of a generous public, which will make him as happy as a *Prince* §.

* An allusion to the masses of snow which were melted in the coppers for a supply of water.

† The individuals engaged in celestial observations, whose *noses* were frequently frost-bitten by coming in contact with the telescopes.

‡ Heated shot that were employed to warm the officers' cabins.

§ Names of the dogs on board the Hecla.

‖ The mallemuke, or fulmar petrel, a bird very common in the Polar Sea.

To the EDITOR of the WINTER CHRONICLE.

SIR—I send you the following lines which were picked up the other evening, between the two ships. Although I cannot claim them as my own, I hope nevertheless to be permitted to sign myself

A CONTRIBUTOR.

Sick of the dullness of the times
I sat me down, to write some rhymes;
'T' avert the shaft ironical
Of writers in the *Chronicle*
'Gainst every sinning, luckless wight,
Who, tho' they can, yet will not write;
But, lack-a-day! my muse is dumb,
And " dinner" calls!—I come! I come!

Our correspondent, with whose contribution we have been much amused, will perceive the alteration of a single word which we have been compelled to make in the lines which he has picked up. We are quite aware how much we have sacrificed to a sense of propriety.

For the WINTER CHRONICLE.

LINES SUGGESTED BY THE BRILLIANT AURORA, JAN. 15, 1820.

HIGH quiv'ring in the air, as shadows fly,
The northern lights adorn the azure sky.
Dimm'd by superior blaze, the stars retire,
And heav'n's vast concave gleams with sportive fire.
Soft blazing in the east, the orange hue,
The crimson, purple, and ethereal blue,
Form a rich arch, by floating clouds upheld
High poised in air, with awful mystery swell'd;
From whose dark centres, with unceasing roll
Rich coruscations gild the glowing pole.
Their varied hues, slow waving o'er the bay,
Eclipse the splendour of the dawning day.
Streamers in quick succession o'er the sky
From the Arc's centre far diverging fly;
Pencils of rays, pure as the heaven's own light,
Dart rapid upward to the zenith s height.

Transfix'd with wonder on the frozen flood,
The blaze of grandeur fired my youthful blood;

Deep in th o'erwhelming maze of Nature's laws,
'Midst her mysterious gloom, I sought the cause;
But vain the search! inscrutable to man
Thy works have been, O God! since time began,
And still shall be.—Then let the thought expire ;
As late the splendours of Aurora's fire
To dark oblivion sank, in wasting flame;
Like the dim shadows of departed fame !   J.

The Editor having presented a box of Bramah's pens to one of the gentlemen who have been called his " Devils," presumes that the following lines are designed as a return:

To the EDITOR of the WINTER CHRONICLE.

I.

Dear Sir, your generosity
Display'd without pomposity,
Impells with new velocity
        Of gratitude the strain.

II.

Such kindness in replenishing
The pens, your papers finishing
Is ev'ry week diminishing,
        Enhances my esteem.

III.

Philosopher's profundity,
Or sparkling wit's fecundity,
Or citizen's rotundity,
        They each may yet record.

IV.

North Georgian geology,
Improvements in conchology,
Or touches of dog-ology,
        Or more upon my word.

V.

Nay, fond attempts poetical,
Opinions hypothetical,
And systems theoretical,
        May by their nibs be traced.

VI.

I 'm prouder in possessing them,
When on the paper pressing them,
Than was the goose when dressing them,
    Whose buoyant wings they graced.

VII.

Mr. Editor, adieu !
Believe me very true
And faithfully your friend,
Until your pens shall end ;
    And now of rhyme
    Enough this time,—
    At wit a nibbler,
    I am

                A Scribbler.

It has given us great pleasure to perceive a considerable increase in the number of our correspondents during the last week. To all of these our acknowledgments are due, but particularly to the author of the "Lines suggested by the Aurora Borealis." This production we do not hesitate to pronounce at once extremely descriptive and highly poetical ; we congratulate our readers on such an acquisition to our Poets' Corner.

THE
NORTH GEORGIA GAZETTE,

PER·FRETA·HACTENUS·NEGATA.

AND
WINTER CHRONICLE.

N°. XV.—MONDAY, FEBRUARY 7, 1820.

To the Editor *of the* Winter Chronicle.

MR. EDITOR,

THE promptness with which the Committee of Management attended to the suggestions contained in my last letter, touching our Theatrical Amusements, afforded me much gratification and pleasure, and has produced a full conviction on my mind that they are actuated by no other motive than a sincere desire to do their best for the public amusement. Having, in some degree, staked my credit on the success which should attend the reproduction of some of the former pieces, you may readily suppose I took my station among the audience at our Theatre, on Wednesday Evening last, with no little share of anxiety for the result, and you will as readily enter into the lively and pleasurable sensations which arose on seeing my most sanguine expectations exceeded. The generality of our audience, Mr. Editor, are not blessed with very quick comprehensions, or clear understandings; and many of the most amusing speeches in a play pass unnoticed on a first representation: the general plot, however, impresses itself on their minds, and prepares them to enter more fully into the spirit of the piece on a second performance, when nearly all the sly jokes, that before escaped their notice, burst upon them, and the entertainment afforded is consequently much greater than before   I was also much pleased, Mr. Editor, in remarking that the Characters, without a single exception, were supported with much greater animation than before, and that the whole piece was conducted with more propriety and spirit than any former representation on our stage.

The gentlemen were evidently actuated by one common feeling, the desire to afford amusement, and in this they succeeded. The conviction that such were their motives, caused me to blush for my own want of exertion, and made me resolve that, in the event of our being called upon to beguile the dull hours of another winter in these regions, I would be amongst the first, in endeavouring to promote so laudable a design; and, that after this season, Mr. Editor, I would no longer remain

A LOOKER-ON.

_____

To the EDITOR *of the* Winter Chronicle.

____

MR. EDITOR,

AFTER a very short absence, on Monday morning last I met with one of my younger children; but to my surprise and grief, its features were so much altered and mutilated, (in consequence of unskilful treatment,) by the small-pox, or some other dreadful malady, that I could scarcely recognise the poor little innocent. My feelings were so shocked by the appalling sight, that it was some time before I regained my usual serenity.

On recovering a little from my confusion, I determined on laying my case before your readers, through the medium of your paper, that they might adopt proper measures for guarding against a similar misfortune.

Don't you think, Mr. Editor, there is a defect in our legislature, and there might, and ought to be, some law enacted for punishing the miscreants, who, under pretence of mending the constitutions of their patients, torture and mangle them to death?

I am, Sir,

Your most obedient Servant,

ANNE ANTI-SCALP.

Had our fair correspondent omitted her signature, and concealed her sex, we might have been so much misled as to suppose her letter alluded to an alteration which we felt ourselves compelled to make in the lines inserted in our last paper, and which were sent to us as having been found between the two ships.

But as the alteration was then acknowledged, and as the result of necessity, not as a supposed improvement; as it was, in fact, the correction of a slip of such a nature, that we are persuaded no female pen would have made, we are driven from this interpretation; however much we might desire to avoid the alternative, of being wholly at a loss to discover the lady's meaning; perhaps our readers may be more successful, and as we have already had experience of their ingenuity in solving enigmas, we solicit their assistance.

_____

THEATRICAL REPORT.

____

We feel, if it be possible, even more satisfaction in noticing the effect which the second representation of *Miss in her Teens* has produced, than when we had the pleasure of congratulating our readers on its success, as the opening piece of our Theatre.

If we were then of opinion that it was desirable to establish such sources of amusement, experience of their beneficial tendency has since far more fully convinced us how important it is that they should be continued. We were early apprized by the Manager that his stock of plays was very limited, and when we saw the indifferent piece of *Bon Ton* given out for representation, it was too evident that but little choice remained; we viewed, therefore, the repetition of a piece already acted as an experiment, on the success of which the continuance of our Theatrical Entertainments essentially depended.

As such we could not but feel anxious during the performance, and although we were amongst those who anticipated that several plays would gain, rather than lose, by repetition (chiefly for reasons which are assigned by our correspondent, " a Looker-on,") we were highly pleased to find that the interest of the audience exceeded rather than fell short of our expectations. Of the attractions and fascinations of novelty none can be unaware ; and did we possess the means of bringing out a succession of new and suitable pieces, it is probable that there would be no question as to the expediency of doing so ; and that the additional trouble that they would occasion, would be but little regarded by the gentlemen who have so cheerfully and diligently exerted themselves to lighten the tediousness of our winter. Repetition might then (if it ever took place) have been confined to plays which had given a more than ordinary pleasure on their first performance.

But if we have been rightly informed that the choice of the managing committee has been divided between the measure which they ultimately adopted, and the desire to undertake one of the three remaining plays, *The Beaux Stratagem, The Suspicious Husband,* or *The World,*—that in their zeal to attempt whatever it might be possible to effect, they did actually for a time contemplate the performance of one of these plays, until experience of the absolute inadequacy of their means obliged them to relinquish it ; if such be indeed the case, we do not hesitate to consider them entitled to the public thanks for adhering to the principle of novelty as long as it could well be maintained. We express this opinion in the perfect recollection that the resources of the theatre have been found competent to do full justice to the only five-act play which has been attempted. But the *Bold Stroke for a Wife,* differs essentially from the three plays above-mentioned ; it depends upon the skill and exertions of a single actor, and in this respect we are not deficient : whereas the other plays, independently of much difficulty in scenery and decorations, would require a greater number of competent actors, much above par, both for the male, as well as female parts, than our theatre can produce. We do not fear censure in making this avowal ; we are persuaded that we do no more than justice to the majority, at least, of the performers, in believing that they do not overrate their own qualifications ; that they are actors, not from choice, but from a sense of duty ; a consideration which would alone have induced many amongst them to place themselves in situations, in which it can be no possible discredit to them to say, Nature did not design them to excel, nor would inclination have ever prompted them to make the attempt.

Theatre Royal, North Georgia.

ON WEDNESDAY, FEBRUARY 16, 1820,

Will be repeated the much-admired Comedy of

THE LIAR;

With the usual accompaniments of SONGS between the Acts.

Fashionable Arrival in North Georgia.

On Thursday last, about noon, after an absence of three months, arrived at his seat, Snow-Hill, in the Isle of White, the Earl of Sol, Viscount Caloric, well known as one of those distinguished luminaries which seem born to enlighten and adorn the world. His lordship has been on his travels in the south, during the winter, accompanied by a numerous retinue of faithful adherents, who could not bear the thought of being separated for so long a period from their illustrious benefactor. Many of these are such fine bucks in their appearance, and have such fawning manners, that into whatever country they go, they are generally made game of; and yet, in spite of this, they are always deer to those who know them.

It is said that his lordship's protracted absence has been severely felt in this neighbourhood, and that it has even produced a considerable degree of coolness between him and his tenants in this country; but as it is well known that his lordship possesses the peculiar quality of imparting his own warmth of heart and melting disposition, to all who are fortunate enough to be placed within the sphere of his genial influence, little doubt can be entertained of a speedy reconciliation.

His lordship is already on his way to the metropolis, but intends travelling by easy journeys, not exceeding twenty miles a day. His noble sister, Lady Luna, has set out to meet him.

FASHIONABLE INTELLIGENCE.

We understand the Earl and Countess of Musk-Ox, Lord and Lady Deer, with their families, are shortly expected from the continent. It is supposed they will not stay long in the metropolis, as they intend passing the summer on their estates in the interior.

We also hear several other persons of distinction are to arrive early in the spring. Among these are the gallant Admiral Lord Glaucus, Colonel Swan, Major Goose, with their amiable ladies, who start immediately for the Lakes; the Hon. Captain Mallemuke, R. N., Sir Eider and Lady Duck, whose accouchement is expected to take place shortly after. The Arch-Duke Bruin is recovering from his late attack of somnolency, and will soon be able to venture out. We are concerned to state that the Prince has been suffering severely from the toothach, and that all the fine teeth which added so much to his expressive countenance are in a rapid state of decay.

The celebrated Mr. Fox, we are informed, has offered to dispose of the valuable chain and collar which he brought away with him on his recent escape from the enemy.

It is with infinite pain we announce the sad accident which befel Lady Georgiana de Loup, after her return the other night from Don Carlo's concert*. Her ladyship was just going to sit down to a light supper, when she placed her foot upon something which severely lacerated it. Doctor Nature was immediately called in, whose eminent skill is, we are happy to hear, likely soon to restore her ladyship to the fashionable world.

Great apprehensions are entertained for that amiable and distinguished nobleman Don Carlo, who has for some time absented himself from his disconsolate friends. His spirits were observed to decline very much ever since the affair mentioned in our last, and it is greatly feared that the malignant aspersions of his enemies have induced him to elope.

---

* An allusion to a wolf which about this time was caught by the foot in a trap, but succeeded in getting away, although severely hurt.

For the WINTER CHRONICLE.

_____

AN INVITATION TO THE FEATHERED RACE.

COME, ye northern fly-aways,
Meet the sun's returning rays ;
Little awks and dovekies too,
Try what our good shots can do ;
Looms and stormy mallemukes,
Flocks of young and tender ducks,
Stoutly for the honour vie
Of a stew, or good sea-pie !
Think, affording such a treat,
How we 'll praise you when we eat !
   King of all the plumy train
Of the Hyperborean main *,
Down whose throat, when wanting prey,
Hapless ducklings find their way ;
Well I know, when nicely drest
You can please a city guest.
Come ! for happy are their fates
Who are smoking on our plates,
Tomb'd your well-pick'd bones shall lie
Deep beneath your native sky,
And your royal skin we 'll stuff,
These are glories great enough !
   Next advance, ye stately geese,
How I long to break the peace,
And my appetite to pall
With your breast, legs, wings, and all !
Come, my wishes realize,
Feast my palate and my eyes.
Dull and formal owls, away,
You, as useless things, may stay :
Yet your skins I won't refuse,
Men of science to amuse.
Come ! but only two or three,
That will surely plenty be !
All the rest of feather'd race,
Prone to flight or rapid chase,
'Midst the Arctic icy sea,
Come or stay—your will is free.

* The glaucous gull, little inferior in size to an eagle.

Boatswains who can't pipe to grog,
'Long with us shall never jog.
And those little squealing brats,
Tern, are only fit for bats;
Kittiwakes and ice-gulls too,
I 'll no powder waste on you.
Go among the whalers' prey,
Full you 're pleased—and so are they.
Puffins, ugly, useless things,
Ne'er among us ply your wings.
But, ye sav'ry land-birds, haste,
Tit-bits for a pamper'd taste!
Partridges, delicious food!
And snow-buntings, small, but good,
Dotterels, and all the lot
Which I've omitted or forgot;
Plume your wings, and seek once more
Northern Georgia's barren shore,
Now become the haunt of man,
And we 'll shoot you—if we can.

QUINTILIAN QUERULOUS.

For the WINTER CHRONICLE.

LINES ON THE RE-APPEARANCE OF THE SUN.

THE splendid sun, with re-ascending ray,
Sheds o'er the northern world the flood of day.
Lost in the blazing radiance, sable night
Resigns her empire to the kindling light.
Serenely clear the heaven's blue concave glows,
And glitt'ring sunshine gilds the mountain snows.
Precursive of the general fire, a stream
Of reddish light shoots up its beauteous gleam,
The conscious skies the blushing tint extend,
Till with their azure dye its glories blend.

Such was the infant orb's primeval ray
That rose o'er fair Creation's early day;
Such was the beam that saw the deluge pour
O'er all the guilty world an ocean's roar;
And such shall be its blaze thro' lasting time,
Till o'er the earth consuming fires shall climb,

Till that Almighty Voice that bade it rise,
Shall blot its glory from the burning skies !

When day's returning light illumes the pole,
Life's crimson streams in swifter currents roll.
Nor man alone the cheerful joy partakes,
The shaggy bear his savage den forsakes ;
The various beasts that haunt the piny wood—
The hardy people of the northern flood—
The sportive birds that skim along in air,
Or on the liquid surface seek their fare,
Return from milder climes, by instinct taught,
Where shelter from the wintry blast they sought ;
All nature feels the life-inspiring ray,
The herbs revive—the ice dissolves away.
Its wonted spring the active mind regains,
No gloomy scene its energy restrains ;
But, as the renovated solar light
Impels the ling'ring shades to rapid flight,
More clearly shine the intellectual pow'rs,
To loftier thoughts the soul aspiring towers.

Man with the sun his upward course pursues
While vig'rous youth his daily force renews ;
Like him, when wasting age those fires consume,
Declining, sinks to death's untravell'd gloom !
May we, like him, before the final scene,
Enlarge our lustre, splendid, yet serene ;
And, as his glowing disk with soften'd light
Still paints the skies when sunk beneath our sight,
In bright remembrance long unfading shine,
By Sovereign Mercy saved, and Love Divine.

THE
NORTH GEORGIA GAZETTE,

PER·FRETA·HACTENUS·NEGATA·

AND
WINTER CHRONICLE.

Nᵒ. XVI.—MONDAY, FEBRUARY 14, 1820.

To the EDITOR of the Winter Chronicle.

Sir,

I do not know whether you take cognizance of such matters as I am now to address you upon; but if you do, I hope you will endeavour to remedy the grievance I complain of. However improbable it may seem to you in these times of somnolency I like to read for an hour or two now and then, and even to write a little occasionally, beyond the daily repetition of " moderate breezes and cloudy," and the formal assertion that we have been " employed as necessary."

Under these circumstances, added to the great scarcity of light in our own cabins at this season, you will, I am certain, enter into my feelings of annoyance, at the innumerable disturbances to which our tables are subject; I allude to the habits which some members of our community have acquired in earlier life, and which they continue to practise daily, to the interruption of the more industrious, and to the absolute preclusion of all serious occupation. I have endeavoured to class these annoyances, or rather those who practise them, under separate heads, of which the first are the *Whistlers*, who, having a tolerable ear themselves, seem to forget that the rest of us have any ears at all, and are continually serenading us with " Molly, put the Kettle on," or the " Duke of York's March," with variations, to the utter discomfiture of every reader within hearing. Of the Whistlers there are frequently more than one, and in that case the process is as follows: Whistler the first (whom I shall call A,) commences a tune: Whistler the second (B,) takes it up about the third or fourth bar, and accompanies him to the end of the stave, by which time A has exhausted his wind, and stopt to replenish his lungs. In the meantime B continues, and just as you are flattering yourself with a hope that *he* also will soon be winded, and allow you to pursue your employments, a third Whistler (C) at the other end of the table, unexpectedly opens his pipes, and takes a spell at the bellows ; soon after which A once more joins the concert with renewed vigour,—and so on *ad libitum*.

Second are the *Hummers*, who are closely allied to the first class, and are distinguished by employing the greater part of the day in humming songs, which they usually do out of tune, and *always* out of time. They are in general more sentimental than the Whistlers in their selection of tunes, confining themselves to the Irish melodies, or some plaintive Scotch ditty. Of these they will hum you a detached bar or two occasionally, in the most pathetic strain imaginable, and are particularly fond of filling up in this manner all the little intervals of time, which are not easily disposed of in any other way, such as while the ink is drying on one side of the paper, or while they are mending their pens, or warming their fingers : perhaps, Mr. Editor, you can recommend some mode of proceeding, by which it shall necessarily fall out that all our pens want mending, and all our fingers warming, exactly at the same instant. We could then all have our *hum* at the same time, and no disturbance would result, as at present, to any individual of the party.

The third class are the *Drummers*, who, to borrow a well-known joke from Joe Miller, were certainly born to make a great noise in the world. They have, like the Whistlers, a tolerable ear for music, and occupy a great deal of their time in drumming most musically with both hands upon the table ; they usually join the Whistlers,

to whom they may, indeed, be considered as an accompaniment. They have been lately practising a new mode of drumming, which is performed by placing the wrist upon the table, and then bringing the nails of each finger, beginning with the little one, in quick succession, one after the other, upon the wood, or what is considered more sonorous and musical, upon a hard-covered book, which they keep by them *shut* for the purpose. I beg leave strongly to recommend this mode, as infinitely more neat and gentleman-like than the other, which consists in merely thumping the table unmercifully with both hands, like a common drummer, and making the candlesticks and inkstands dance a horn-pipe. Perhaps these first three classes might be employed with advantage for a couple of hours daily, in whistling, humming, and drumming to the ships' companies, when they take exercise : and a convenient spot for practising their arts might be selected in the neighbourhood of the boat-house, or the green ravine.

Fourth in order are the *Bangers*, who never bring a book or a desk, or any thing else to the table, without banging it down with all their might and main, to the sad derangement of all weak nerves, and the production of many an unintentional pot-hook in their neighbour's writing. This practice would seem intended to announce the arrival of the said Bangers, as if they had exclaimed, " Behold, I say ! I am actually going to write !" Such an event which, it must be confessed, is singular enough in itself, and of vital importance to us all, might, I should think, be announced with full as much effect, and with much less disturbance to others, by all the Bangers being furnished with a conical cap and bells, such as is described to have been worn by Counsellor Puzzlewell on a certain occasion ; the jingle of the bells would give ample notice of their approach, and save our table many a lusty thump, which even the strongest of them cannot stand without shaking.

The fifth class consists of the *Blowers,* so called from the frequency with which they blow their noses, when nature requires no such operation. By constant practice they have attained such perfection in that noisy art, that it is now really a public nuisance. It resembles the sound of a ferryman's conch, or a news-boy's horn, and being repeated at regular and mechanical intervals, completely distracts your attention. There is a custom on board some of our ships, of sending buglemen to practise at the bowsprit-end, that they may not disturb anybody else. The same situation would be an eligible one for these unnatural and preposterous nose-blowers, who might there be indulged in their propensity to pull their own noses, without annoying their neighbour's ears. Having already exceeded the limits of a letter, I am under the necessity of concluding, without having half finished my list, and shall, perhaps, resume the subject at some future time, should I see occasion to do so. In the meanwhile I remain, Mr. Editor,

Your obedient Servant,

Z.

BIRTHS.

On Sunday morning last, at her residence near Culinary Range, Bed-place-square, the lady of Sir Thomas Mousewell, of a son and daughter. Surprising as it may appear, it is nevertheless an undoubted fact, that these infants were endowed with the power of walking immediately on their birth, while both were totally unable to see. We are concerned to state, that a fatal accident occurred in consequence, as the former having rambled to the entrance of the apartment, was so severely bruised by an attendant shutting the door hastily, that it expired the same evening. Lady M. and her daughter are doing well, and great hopes are indulged, that in a few days the latter will enjoy perfect sight.

DOMESTIC INTELLIGENCE, &c.

On Monday last, that well-known many-headed monster, the *Encea Borealis,* vulgarly called N. C., was caught in a trap, and firmly tied down with strong lashings. This animal is not described by Linnæus, nor by any other naturalist, and is now generally supposed to be peculiar to North Georgia. The attempts which, for at least fifteen weeks past, have been made to secure him, have, we are happy to find, at length succeeded, and the public may congratulate themselves on their deliverance from this monster, whose attacks at one time seemed to threaten serious injury to the community. The first accounts concerning him, state him to have had seven or eight heads, and as many tongues ; some of these were very venomous, while others only snarled and growled, and were perfectly harmless.

The manner in which these heads, &c., have been gradually got rid of, is remarkable enough : it was accidentally discovered that a certain composition, with which it was customary to bait the traps every Monday morning, had the extraordinary effect of destroying animation, in a short time, in one or more of the heads ; so that, by repeated doses of the same nature, they have nearly all dropped off one by one, and the animal may now be considered perfectly harmless and inoffensive.

STANZAS

ON THE DEATH OF A FAVOURITE SETTER DOG.

———

I.

Farewell, poor Carlo! hapless dog, adieu!
  We mourn thy fate unknown *; but fate too sure;
For fled is ev'ry hope that Fancy drew,
  Nor could thy frame the piercing frost endure.

II.

A wilder'd wanderer in the midnight shade,
  Sagacious dog, thou wert not wont to stray;
And long thy wish'd return, tho' still delay'd,
  We vainly look'd for each revolving day.

III.

On these drear plains, exposed to ev'ry blast,
  Thy bones shall whiten in the wintry wind:
For ah! thy generous confidence at last,
  Betray'd thee friendless to the savage kind!

IV.

Lured 'mid the rabid wolf's ferocious train,
  Thy guiltless blood distain'd the fleecy snow;
Indignant courage fired thy heart in vain,
  Yet wert thou not in fight a feeble foe.

V.

Long shall thy mem'ry in each bosom dwell
  That beats to Nature's warm emotions true;
Oft too for thee the rising sigh shall swell,
  And fond regret thy timeless fate pursue.

---

* Poor Carlo continued his daily rambles with the she-wolf until, at length—he went and returned no more. His fate was never ascertained; but there can be little doubt that he fell a
victim in an encounter with the male, as Boatswain, another of our dogs, who was decoyed away
in the same manner a few days afterwards, returned to us after a combat, in which it was evident
he had hardly escaped with life.

VI.

For animation fill'd thy sparkling eye,
  And gentle pleasure every look express'd,
When some loved footstep heard approaching nigh,
  Inspired with joy thy almost reasoning breast.

VII.

Farewell, poor Carlo! tho' no tablet rise
  The frail memorial of thy fatal doom,
Thy faithful worth the generous mind will prize,
  While Winter's gather'd snows adorn thy tomb!

For the WINTER CHRONICLE.

HYPERBOREAN PRIVILEGE.

Young Cupid! fond of unity
Our Boreal community
Defy you with impunity;
    Your arrows and your bow.

This day of sensibility
And Valentine's fertility,
Displays invincibility
    Among the northern snow.

Your daring animosity
Imparts a tremulosity,
And winds its sinuosity
    Around each beating heart;

That beauty, smiling graciously
Altho' perhaps fallaciously,
But catching one incautiously,
    Will make it sorely smart.

But no universality
Attends on this formality,
Without congeniality
    Of sun-beams, groves, and bowers.

o

Here Sol obliquely glittering,
Prevents the bosoms twittering,
That pert young ladies tittering
    Attribute to your powers.

Blest with inflexibility
To bright eyes and gentility,
We owe no liability
    Of being hurt by you.

'Tis pity man so spirited
Should bear such ill unmerited,
And be so sadly ferretted
    By passion strong and true.

Almost devoid of covering,
In southern climes stay hovering,
The cold would set you shivering,
    So urchin boy, adieu !

For o'er our hearts you must your pow'r resign,
Till we returning bow at Beauty's shrine.

TO CORRESPONDENTS.

The communications from A. T. and Constantine Cataplasm have been received.

Peter Pastoral is too lofty for our comprehension.

The Lady who quarrels with her husband must excuse us if we decline interfering in a case so delicate.

Peter Query is under consideration.

The hint given by our friend M. will be attended to.

THE

NORTH GEORGIA GAZETTE,

AND

WINTER CHRONICLE.

No. XVII.—MONDAY, FEBRUARY 21, 1820.

To the EDITOR *of the* Winter Chronicle.

SIR,

The melancholy event which happened on Friday on board the Hecla, I mean the non-cookery of our pies in proper time for dinner, has given rise to some reflections, which, as the matter concerns us all alike, may not be uninteresting to your readers.

It was truly distressing to see the long and woe-begone faces to which this unusual and unexpected occurrence gave rise. One member had just warmed and rubbed his hands, and then declared that he was " quite ready," when it was announced on authority that could not be disputed, that the pies were not quite so ready; in short, that a whole hour at least must elapse before the said pies, or any substitute for them, could possibly be brought to table.

It often, I believe, happens that the half hour which precedes the announcement of dinner is an insipid one rather than otherwise; but how would it be possible to give an adequate idea of the horror of the whole hour, which preceded ours on Friday last! Innumerable schemes were resorted to, to wile away the tedious interval; the Hummers, Drummers, and Whistlers went to work in their respective branches of discord, and this for the first quarter of an hour seemed to succeed to admiration. Then the dog was plagued and the fire poked; and then the dog plagued again, but all in vain! Neither poking, nor plaguing, nor humming, nor drumming, were ever known to satisfy the cravings of hunger such as ours. At length an expedient was happily hit upon. " Tir'd Nature's sweet restorer, balmy sleep," as the poet has it, stept into our relief, and hunger and thirst were in an instant forgotten.

I doubt whether history can produce another such instance as this of cheerful resignation, and heroic fortitude! Amidst all the hardships which we have been called upon to suffer, none, Mr. Editor, has equalled this. And how did our gallant comrades conduct themselves under this affliction? Let it ever be recorded to their immortal renown, that they patiently bowed down their heads under the stroke, and instead of murmurs and complaints, nothing but— snores were heard till dinner arrived.

Little do they think at home, Mr. Editor, what we have been, and are still, undergoing for our country's sake! Little do they think that we have only as much to eat as we can conveniently stuff into our maws, and that as one of your early correspondents remarks, we can only " snatch our ten hours' rest at night!" How would their heart sink within them, could they be told, that once in nine months we have been reduced to the heart-breaking alternative of going without our dinner, or of roughing it upon half a pound of fresh meat, ditto bread, with all the little supplementary *etceteras* of cheese, brandy, lemon-juice and wine, with which his Majesty has been graciously pleased to supply us!

Snore on, ye adventurous youths, ye " marine worthies!" continue to display this magnanimous self-devotion, and you will not fail to meet a rich reward from a generous and grateful country!

I am, Sir,
Your most obedient Servant,
A SPECTATOR.

———

To the Author of the Letter signed Z in last Week's Chronicle.

———

MY DEAR MR. Z—As you gave us to understand in the last Chronicle, that you intended to continue your account of the different annoyances to which our tables are exposed, I write to beg you will not forget the " Door-slammers," who have been for months past a daily and hourly inconvenience to

Your obedient Servant,
X.

———

To the EDITOR of the Winter Chronicle.

———

SIR—Being encouraged by the manner in which my last meteorological communication was received by you and your readers, I venture once more to intrude myself upon your columns, and trust I shall, on this occasion, receive credit for the same public-spirited intentions by which my former letter was dictated. My present purpose is somewhat similar, it being my desire to correct an error which has somehow or other crept into the heads of some members of our community, respecting the actual temperature of the atmosphere on the 15th of this month. My observations on this important subject were carried on with the same instruments, and the same care, as before; and I do assure your readers that 54 degrees and 984 thousandth parts below zero was all I could conscientiously screw out by hook or by crook. I hope, therefore, that those who have marked 55° in their journals will immediately cause so gross a mistake to be rectified, especially as my extensive reading on philosophical subjects has enabled me to ascertain, since I last addressed you, that a natural temperature of — 57° has actually been before registered; so that unless the sticklers for our frigorific fame can manage to suggest some mode of escaping such eternal infamy, we must rest content under the dreadful certainty of having been outshivered by others, the enormous quantity of two degrees and forty-six thousandth parts. I am sorry that I cannot assist these gentlemen in their laudable designs, and remain as before,

Your obedient Servant,
SIMON SET-RIGHT.

***

THEATRICAL REPORT.

ON Wednesday last was performed for the second time this season, the comedy of *The Liar*.

The extreme coldness of the night, and the impossibility of keeping the theatre at a comfortable temperature, deprived the audience of much of the gratification which they have hitherto received from our theatrical amusements, and which the unremitted exertions of the performers would otherwise have ensured.

***

Theatre Royal, North Georgia.

On WEDNESDAY, MARCH 1, 1820.

Will be repeated the much admired Farce of

THE CITIZEN.

After which

THE MAYOR OF GARRATT.

The doors will open at Half past Six, and the Performance commence precisely at Seven o'Clock.

***

For the WINTER CHRONICLE.

***

I SAT me down with firm intent
  To write for the Gazette,
But soon the cold my fingers bent,
  And made me fume and fret.

My great coat then I button'd up,
  Put my night-cap on my head,
Of coffee took another cup,
  And ate some toasted bread.

Then with the poker stirr'd the fire,
  Which speedily burnt clearer,
Put on some coals to make it higher,
  And drew my chair in nearer.

My fingers still were cold as lead,
　My toes with pain were smarting,
My teeth kept chattering in my head,
　And life seem'd fast departing.

When, notwithstanding this sad plight,
　My subject I had chosen,
Produced my paper fair and white,
　Behold ! my ink was frozen !

Adzooks, quoth I, this ne'er will do,
　The matter's very clear,
One cannot write with any goût,
　In such an atmosphere.

I therefore beg, good Mr. E,
　You will excuse a letter,
And publish my apolo—gy
　For want of something better.

　　　　　　　　　　　　　　Q.

———

To the EDITOR of the WINTER CHRONICLE.

—

Sir, having met
In your Gazette
Some lines that plainly shew,
　That all should write
　And send their mite,
No matter sense or no.

I muster'd strength,
And strove at length
To jingle words together,
　But 'twas no joke
　For any folk
To write in such cold weather.

So thought my Muse,
Who did not choose
T' impart ideas clear,
　But did uphold
　That 't was too cold
For her to tarry here.

In truth, I said,
My gentle maid
The case is clear you see,
If I don't write,
And that this night,
They 'll class me with N. C.

Why, that 's no matter,
Hold your chatter,
I 'm not now in the cue :
When it grows mild
I 'll help you, child,
Till then I bid adieu.

MEREDITH MAKESHIFT.

THE
NORTH GEORGIA GAZETTE,

AND
WINTER CHRONICLE.

Nº. XVIII—MONDAY, FEBRUARY 28, 1820.

To the EDITOR *of the* Winter Chronicle.

SIR,

In performance of the promise made to you and your readers in your last Number but one, I continue my account of the several annoyances by which our tables have been long visited; and I beg at the same time to offer you my acknowledgments for the part you have taken towards their eradication, by inserting a letter of such unconscionable length as my last, in your gazette. The class standing next upon my list is that of the Snorers, who are upon the whole, so inoffensive a set, that it almost goes to my heart to hold them up to public notice. There is, moreover, some danger, lest by doing any thing to break them of snoring, they might also be prevented from sleeping; and this would be an irreparable injury to our community, because, whilst in this state, they are certainly much less annoyance to us than when wide awake; for you must know, Mr. Editor, that these same snorers, as soon as they open their eyes, are generally converted, as if by magic, into hummers or drummers, or some other of the noisy classes I have before described. Rather, therefore, than be the means of robbing our tables of one hour's quiet during the day, by finding fault with so laudable a practice as that of sleeping, I shall dismiss this part of the subject with expressing a hope that some means may be suggested of teaching these gentlemen to sleep without snoring. Perhaps it might be of some service to have attached to each of them a flapper, such as we are told by Gulliver, the great people in Laputa have. I dare say the marines could easily be trained to this: they should be instructed to give them a good smart box on the ear at every snore, and then to smooth them down, to re-compose them to sleep, taking particular care, which a few days' practice would enable them to do, to make them feel the blow pretty sharply, but by no means to run the risk of absolutely awakening them.

I now come to the Sniffers, who, by some means or other, have got out of their place in my catalogue, as they ought to have followed the Blowers; because, like those, the offence they give is chiefly by the nose.

They are, however, in one essential point, the very reverse of the blowers; because, whereas these last are always using their pocket-handkerchiefs, the Sniffers never use any, but perform the same office more economically, more frequently, and I must in justice add, with less disturbance to others than those tremendous Conch-Blowers. The Sniffers have been observed to increase very much since the last cold weather set in, and there is, perhaps, some excuse for them; but I do hereby give notice that all Sniffing, after the 10th of March, must be considered absolutely inadmissible; and the Sniffers are hereby required, in the mean time, to provide themselves with a proper number of handkerchiefs, and to blow their noses like gentlemen, after that date, on pain of being posted for the non-performance of the same in the succeeding week's newspaper.

Next in order on my list I find the Slammers, or as my correspondent X. has denominated them, the Door-Slammers. These, Mr. Editor, are indeed as Mr. X. has expressed it, " a daily and hourly inconvenience." But alas! what chance can any effort of mine have of correcting this noisy practice, when even a civil request publickly made by the commander of the expedition to have mercy on his own door, and the adjoining bulk-heads, has not yet had any perceptible effect? It is not necessary for me to

explain in what the art of the Slammers consists, for the word must at once convey to our minds, what our ears are so constantly in the habit of experiencing. But there are some circumstances attending the practice of this art, which my constant observation has made me acquainted with, and which your readers will, upon trial, find to be correct.

It may be relied on as an incontrovertible fact, that the force with which the Slammers shut the doors, is intended by them, as by the Bangers, to announce their arrival; for, without some such means, so important an event might possibly remain unnoticed, and for this they would never forgive themselves. Some of the more inveterate of this class, after they have slammed the door with becoming energy, on entering stand awhile to assure themselves that all hands are made aware of their coming; and then, and not till then, complacently take their seats. It has often been remarked, Mr. Editor, that little people are more consequential than those who are taller. Whether this be the case or not, I will not pretend to determine; but certain I am that, with very few exceptions, the great people of our community slam the doors the hardest, and the little-great people the hardest of all. Indeed so exactly proportional have I generally found the slam of the door to be to the size of the person, and according to the popular notion, to his consequence also, that I would be bound to guess a man's height within an inch or so, by the manner in which he shuts the door. Perhaps, if you knew my own size, you would allow that I have, in the following description, sacrificed all personal feeling to a sense of justice and truth. Your King-John's man, commonly said to measure four feet nothing, enters with a tremendous slam,—like Jove he carries his thunder about with him! A neat dapper little fellow of five feet three or four inches makes the bulkheads quake again, and what is even worse, by his ill-managed violence, causes the door to re-open, so that he stuns and freezes you at the same time. As we get to five feet six, and from that to five feet ten, the doors are shut more moderately; and a decent sized fellow, of near six feet or upwards, even of considerable consequence, may go in and out of an apartment and scarcely be heard. I know of one way, and only one, in which the Slammers can possibly be cured of their habit. I have heard of a dog having been broke of worrying a cat by muzzling him, and then letting pussy scratch his nose in security. My recipe for the Slammers is of the same kind. Let their heads be securely and closely tied to the most rattling door in either ship, then let two stout men, one on each side, be employed for an hour in opening and shutting the door, as often and as hard as they are able. If this dose taken three times a day, for one week, does not cure the most inveterate case in the history of this disease, the Slammers may indeed be pronounced absolutely incorrigible.

I now come to the Growlers, a very teasing class, of whom I had a good deal to say, but I find I have been anticipated by a more satirical writer in your last gazette, who took occasion to descant on this subject, when, lamentable to relate! the pies on board the Hecla, were not cooked in proper time for dinner. As your correspondent " A Spectator," may have it in contemplation to resume this fertile subject at a future time, I shall very willingly leave it in his hands, and as I fancy you and your readers will begin to think I am again growing tedious, I shall reserve the remainder of my list to some other time ; and I assure you I have yet a choice collection. By way of reporting progress on my last communication, I shall only at present add that one Nose-blower has been reclaimed;

but another is as bad as ever. I have heard two Whistlers stifle their tunes in the middle, and they may therefore be said to be half corrected in their habit.

The Bangers all laugh at my joke ; but one of the principal of them does not put the cap on his own head, for which it was chiefly intended. No amendment is yet perceived in the Hummers or Drummers, and I therefore give notice to the said Hummers and Drummers, that as they are unanimously declared to be the greatest pest, except the Slammers, which our tables have, they must either mend their manners, or expect to be handled more severely in some future communication,

From your obedient Servant,
Z.

To the EDITOR of the Winter Chronicle.

MR. EDITOR.—As I was passing one of the cabins the other day, my ears were saluted by such an extraordinary medley of murmuring sounds, that I could not for the life of me, although averse to such practices, refrain from peeping in. If my wonder was before excited, how much greater was it upon finding the cabin, except its usual furniture and *a red-hot shot*, perfectly empty.

After reflecting a few moments on this curious phænomenon, the enigma was at length solved by my recollecting to have read of some travellers whose voices froze during the winter, and on the return of milder weather formed a similar concert. Being now satisfied that the sounds were caused by the influence of the red-hot shot on the surrounding atmosphere, I entered the cabin, and enjoyed one of the most delightful half hours you can possibly imagine.

The words were uttered, if I may be allowed the expression, in a soft musical cadence, and being lengthened out very much by the gradual process of thawing, and occasionally interspersed with sighs and interjections, produced such wild and soothing harmony, that my senses were soon lulled into a most delicious torpor. The tunes, to be sure, were sometimes broken by harsh and dissonant notes, but for the most part their melody abundantly compensated for those trifling annoyances.

I wish it was in my power to give you an adequate idea of this aërial concert; but as it would be vain to attempt such a task, I shall content myself with subjoining a short specimen of the language, leaving the rest to your imagination.

Resplendent orb!—in shady groves—heigh ho!—bright progeny of Jove—nine times 6 is 54.—The hero fired—fatal charms—Heaven's vast concave—bound in firm ice the fettered ships—pshaw!—flour and suet for 491 days —Mr. Editor—

Soft was the lustre of her heavenly eye,
Like the mild splendour of an arctic sky—

Coals two chaldrons—alas! woe is me—candles—after—hold—Non—Contri—do—fa—

ce." As the shot cooled, the words gradually lengthened, and became incoherent; then were only half expressed; and at length the sound finally ceasing, all was hushed in silence.

It has frequently been the subject of regret with me since, that from the want of talent, I lost so fine an opportunity of furnishing something for the last week's paper; it is, indeed, a pity some others of your correspondents were not present who, by exerting a little of their wonted ingenuity, might soon have collected materials enough for either poetry or prose, and rendered their apologies unnecessary, besides filling the half sheet which the disappointed community was deprived of by the frigidity of the weather.

However, should their wits fail them upon any future occasion, a glowing loggerhead placed in any of the cabins, which probably you can point out, will not fail of supplying abundant store of elegant, witty, and brilliant ideas.

I remain, Mr. Editor,
Your most obedient,
PEEPING TOM.

For the WINTER CHRONICLE.

REFLECTIONS OCCASIONED BY THE FIRE AT THE OBSERVATORY HOUSE, AT
WINTER HARBOUR, FEBRUARY 24th, 1820.

THY mercies, O Eternal King!
　Still guard the creatures of thy pow'r,
Thy glories wond'ring angels sing,
　Thy goodness marks the passing hour.

Dark, formless chaos at thy word
　Submissive into order roll'd,
Thy hand the new creation stored,
　And deck'd the skies with living gold.

Each fleeting moment speaks thy love,
   Our ev'ry pulse proclaims thy grace;
To distant lands if we remove,
   We still thy loving-kindness trace.

When borne upon the northern blast
   Was heard the dismal cry of fire,
A chill thro' ev'ry bosom pass'd,
   A nameless horror, deep and dire.

But hope again each eye illumed,
   'Twas not our ships involved in flame;
The labours of our hands consumed,
   Yet we survive, to praise thy name.

At such a time the scene how dread!
   Keen frost pervading all the air,
Had quickly number'd with the dead
   The few the elements might spare.

Thou Great Supreme, Almighty Lord,
   Preserve us safe from ev'ry ill,
Thy guardian presence still afford,
   And let us taste thy bounty still!

When, at thy nod, the doom-born flame
   Shall burst the womb of ending time,
May Jesu's merit give us claim
   To dwell with Thee in worlds sublime.

LINES SUGGESTED BY THE DEATH OF A GULL,

WHO WAS BURNT IN THE FIRE WHICH BROKE OUT IN THE OBSERVATORY HOUSE

UNHAPPY gull, thy luckless end
   May almost claim a tear;
And thus to all that will attend
   I 'll make the matter clear.

Thy parents on the sea-wash'd beach
   Fell, pierced by fatal lead;
In vain from swift pursuer's reach
   Thyself and brother fled.

What tho' denied aloft to soar,
  Or skim the waters round ;
You both upon North Georgia's shore
  Pea-soup in plenty found.

Yet food affords but small delight
  When squabbles break our rest ;
And John and you would often fight,
  The cause yourselves knew best.

But Johnny died—and this last source
  Of pleasure with him fell,
When dire ennui's all-fretful force
  Did in your bosom swell.

At length the fatal morn arrives,
  Unusual flames ascend ;
Had you possess'd an hundred lives,
  They all had found an end.

I feel, 'tis true, some sense of pain
  Your suff'rings to review ;
But such regrets are ever vain,—
  Miss Jenny Gull—adieu !

For the WINTER CHRONICLE.

A PHILOSOPHIC REVERIE.

Poor tatter'd remnants of my wash,
  Tho' you no more my shoulders grace ;
Vexation would appear so rash,
  I must put on a smiling face.

Some tail-less—frill-less some, I find,
  Some collar-less and arm-less too,
Some quite to tinder scorch'd behind,
  And all will mending want, with new.

Tis very true the shirts are gone,
  But what are they, if safe the skin !
Some skins I 've lost, but there is one
  Yet safe and sound—and that I'm in !

I view'd the blaze, and bit my thumbs,
  Then heaved a scientific sigh ;
But since the clicking pendulums
  Are saved—I'll now to dinner fly.

———————

For the WINTER CHRONICLE.

———

THE EDITOR BE-DEVILLED.

Said Devil the first to his partner one day
  When meeting in office, to set up the type ;
" For once, brother-devil, we 'll have our own way ;
  " So suppose that we give our dear master a wipe."

This made the poor editor look quite demure,
  When he found that their jokes at himself were thus levell'd ;
" Never Editor had two such devils, I 'm sure,
  " For between them, I own myself fairly be-devill'd."

———————

For the WINTER CHRONICLE.

———

The Commander exclaim'd, " What a fine thing is *Peat*
  For making a fire, and giving out heat ;
" That 's true," replied Fur-clad, who by it was seated,
  " I strongly advise you to have it re-*peated.*"

———————

THE
NORTH GEORGIA GAZETTE,

AND
WINTER CHRONICLE.

Nº. XIX—MONDAY, MARCH 6, 1820.

To the EDITOR *of the* Winter Chronicle.

THE cry of Reform having reached even to North Georgia, I shall request of you to exert your interest with Z in my behalf, trusting that the commiseration which my case must excite, will induce him to adopt measures for effecting its speedy amendment. You must know then, that I am very fond of telling a good story, or what is technically called " spinning a yarn;" have doubled the Cape, been at Pulo Penang, Palambang, Tanjong, Goonting, Mangalore, Cannanore, and most of the pulo's, bangs and ores in the Indian and China seas.

What I have to complain of is this— having finished what I believe to be a very marvellous story, up rises one of these gentlemen, whom I shall distinguish by the appellation of a walking phenomenon, who, not having doubled the Cape, is not a privileged man, and relates something similar, but three times more extraordinary, and immediately robs me of that awe and admiration which we Cape men are alone entitled to.

Now, Mr. Editor, I'll leave it to your impartial judgment, whether my case does not deserve notice. Pray, do all you can for me with Z, and use your editorial influence and authority to lay these unqualified wonder-mongers.

I am, Sir,
Your obedient Servant,
NATHAN LONG-BOW.

To the EDITOR *of the* Winter Chronicle.

MY DEAR SIR—Captivated by the delicacy, the exquisite sentiment, and the tenderness for the feelings of others, displayed by the charming Mr. Z., I beg, through your means, to implore the publication of his essays in a separate form, and that my name may be placed at the head of the list of subscribers, to ensure me the estimation of the public, which he has so liberally endeavoured to procure for his companions.

I remain, my dear Sir,
Your ever-obliged
EMILY.

To the Editor *of the* Winter Chronicle.

Mr. EDITOR—Lest you or your readers should think I have any thing to do with your correspondent who has thought proper to assume my signature in your last Number, and who seems to be so well versed in the art of extracting, not only sense, but " abundant store of elegant, witty, and brilliant ideas," from loggerheads, I beg to disclaim all knowledge of or connexion with him, and to subscribe myself as before,

Your obedient Servant,
PEEPING-TOM, THE FIRST.

To the EDITOR *of the* Winter Chronicle.

SIR—Being one of those who have felt it my duty to contribute my mite occasionally towards filling the columns of your Gazette, I have been desirous for these two or three weeks past, to drop something into your box, and have therefore essayed to write an article, but in vain; the severe cold weather which called forth the apologies of your more constant correspondents, in the last Number but one, has so cramped the few ideas which I possess, that I have been rendered totally incapable of producing any thing. Under these circumstances, I became

apprehensive lest the same cause producing similar effects upon our community in general, should leave your pages blank, and deprive us of our usual Monday morning's entertainment. Guess, then, the relief which my anxiety felt on finding this dreaded vacuum so ably filled up by the effusions of " a glowing loggerhead !"

I confess, Mr. Editor, that since my residence in North Georgia, I have been mightily taken with the society of those self-same loggerheads, and have used my best endeavours to obtain them as guests in my cabin as frequently as possible. It is true, they are in general much addicted to *irony,* but when warmed into a proper temper by the neighbourhood of a good coal-fire, they become the most agreeable companions that can be conceived, and I boldly venture to affirm, there is not a man of sense in our whole community who does not feel pleasure in receiving a visit from one of the loggerhead tribe, when their noddles are thus heated to a glowing temperature.

But, Mr. Editor, highly as I appreciate their talents in diffusing warmth and cheerfulness to all who come within the sphere of their genial influence, I could not help expressing the most agreeable surprise on finding that one of them had not only surpassed the rest, but actually outstripped all others of our community by producing " such wild and soothing harmony," as tended to " lull the senses into a most delicious torpor !" Although the cooling process, I presume caused much of the *irony* I have before spoken of, to be mixed up with the wit and good-humour contained in the disjointed sentences which " Peeping Tom" has transcribed, they are, nevertheless, so amusing, that I equally regret with himself, the cause by which he was prevented from giving us more of them. As, however, the ice is broken, the thawing process will, in all probability, continue; and as Peeping-Tom's acquaintance with the Loggerheads who afforded us this aërial concert, will enable him to keep a watch upon them, I hope to see many of your future columns filled by effusions of the same kind, in which (contrary to what might have been reasonably expected,) there is neither perversion of sense, nor inversion of sound, but an excellent substitute for the themes which were " nipp'd i' the bud" by the frigidity of the weather, and which rendered necessary the apologies of so many of your Correspondents, among which I beg may be included

Your obedient Servant,

Tom Peeped-at.

For the WINTER CHRONICLE.

Hyperborean Soporifics.

No sylvan scenes around me lie,
    That can my Muse incite
From famed Parnassian regions high,
    To wing her hasty flight.

But in my cabin's snug recess,
    She sometimes deigns to sit,
Descant upon dark Winter's dress,
    Or sharpen up my wit,

And now I feel the maid inspire
    The concave of my head,
Creating in my brain a fire,
    To sing an Arctic bed.

When from the lagging hours of day
    I hasten to repose,
The cold admits of no delay,
    In taking off my clothes.

Prepared at length, a shiv'ring wight,
    Quick into bed I leap,
And neath six blankets' cumbrous weight,
    Compose myself to sleep.

O'er all to guard from frosty air
    Is stretch'd a wolf's warm hide,
Which I, with more than common care
    Tuck in on either side.

In woollen wrapt o'er head and ears
   I snore till morning-light,
While dreaming fancy often rears
   A scene of past delight.

But at my door the servant stops,
   " Sir, 'tis almost seven bells;"
Then in a light he quickly pops,
   Which every fancy quells.

The drowsy yawn which still precedes
   Ere off our sleep we shake,
Against the ice my elbow leads,
   And shivers me awake.

A moment then in state I lie,
   All thoughts of slumber lost;
While beauteous crystals meet my eye
   In varied works of frost.

Illumined by the candle's rays
   They deck my cabin's top,
But feeling soon the heated blaze
   They liquefy and drop.

O! more than eastern luxury,
   Without the artist's aid,
In shower-bath to mollify,
   At ease so haply laid!

But hark! that noise! each clanging cup
   And saucer rattles round;
The signal heard, I'm quickly up,
   And soon at breakfast found.

PHILO-SOMNUS.

NOTICE TO CORRESPONDENTS.

We have to apologize to our Correspondent Z for the accidental omission in our last week's Paper, of an acknowledgment which we had designed to make, in consequence of having felt ourselves under the necessity of omitting a section of his second communication.

We hope he will favour the Public with his promised continuation.

THE
NORTH GEORGIA GAZETTE,

PER·FRETA·HACTENUS·NEGATA.

AND
WINTER CHRONICLE.

N°. XX—MONDAY, MARCH 13, 1820.

To the EDITOR *of the* Winter Chronicle.

SIR,

The very flattering encouragement which I met with in your last Number, not only from yourself but from two or three of your Correspondents, has made me venture another letter into your box. Authors are naturally as proud of their productions as a mother is of her children; but nobody but authors can conceive the rapture experienced on hearing their works praised by the public, and especially by the softer sex.

Such was the rapture your humble servant Z experienced on reading Emily's short but sweet epistle in your last Gazette. Publish my essays in a separate volume! Dear creature, to be sure I will! What can Z refuse his Emily? Pray, Mr. Editor, endeavour to fish her residence out for me, and she shall have the two first copies that come from the press! But I had almost forgotten my purpose—perhaps woman, charming woman—will be a sufficient apology.

I do not quite understand whether you received a note from me on the subject of the omission of a part of one of my communications, to which omission you have alluded in your last week's paper. In that note, I think, I said that perhaps my communications were too long for your purpose; and, as you have not taken any notice of this, I conclude that you have glanced it over with your usual courtesy, and shall take your hint accordingly, by making this letter of a more moderate length than my former ones. If I do not mistake, some of your readers will be much obliged to me for this new arrangement, by which I shall be obliged to confine myself to a brief description of the

Stampers, a class of people who are distinguished by the loudness and frequency of their stamping when they first enter our apartments, and for some time afterwards. The Stampers may say their toes are cold, but it is no such thing, Mr. Editor, take my word for it. Ten times in eleven that they thus disturb us, their toes are warm enough; besides, if we admit this excuse for the Stampers, I suppose the Drummers will tell us their fingers are cold, and the Snorers that they sleep to keep their eyes warm; at all events I think, the least the Stampers can do, is to have their stamping out on deck, where, during the cold weather, they are certainly privileged to exercise their art to the full extent of their wishes, as long as they keep before the main-mast.

I rather think, however, that if this practice could be banished from our apartments, the sum total of stamping would be much reduced; for, you must know, Mr. Editor, I have reason to suspect that the motive is generally the same as that by which the Bangers, Slammers, &c., are actuated. In short, that it is only another ingenious expedient for announcing to us, in a way which cannot possibly escape notice, the actual arrival of the party concerned.

But it is time for me to report progress. Alas! what progress have I to report! I see no improvement excepting a slight amendment in the *Whistlers*, who, by-the-by, I am sorry to hear, are gaining the languishing sentimental style of the Hummers.

The Drummers indeed, have shewn some signs of a new pest which they are preparing for us; not satisfied with what their fingers can perform upon the tables, I have heard a foot or two at work under them for some time past, by which a sort of tattoo has been produced, almost as melodious as the other. If the Drummers mean to continue this, they ought in common decency, to sit without shoes, that their tapping may not disturb us. The Slammers are worse than ever, but until my remedy has been fairly tried, they must not be pronounced incorrigible. The Snorers snore less, but I fear I have done mischief, for they *sleep* less also.

My compliments to " Nathan Long-bow," and I will take his case into consideration, respecting the *Wonder-mongers*.

If my friend " A Spectator," does not give the *Growlers* a hint or two, it will be a great pity; for, our late *hardships* have brought them out, as a warm sun does the flies in spring.

Best love to Emily, from her constant slave, and

> Your obedient Servant,
>
> Z.

To the EDITOR *of the* Winter Chronicle.

Mr. EDITOR—I have to request you will allow me a short space in your columns, to make the apology to *Peeping-Tom the First*, which the grossness of my offence demands; and I beg to assure him, that when I assumed his title, my secondary right to it was omitted purely from inadvertency, and not from the slightest wish to claim any connexion with him. To tell you the truth, (between ourselves, for I would not have it generally known,) I quite forgot the existence of that pre-eminent personage. *Sic transit gloria mundi.*

> I am, Sir,
> Your most obedient Servant,
> PEEPING-TOM THE SECOND.

To the EDITOR *of the* Winter Chronicle.

Mr. EDITOR—If I was gratified by the

visits which were paid to our ships this time last year, when in the river, how much more so was I in this desolate place, to meet my friend Sir Partial Thaw, under the stern on Tuesday last. I gave him an invitation to stay, but he said that he regretted his visit must be short, for he was obliged to attend in other places; and, while he assured me that it was with great reluctance he left us, he was so deeply affected, that the natural warmth and goodness of his heart over-flowed, and trickled down upon the snow. He had been upon the lower deck, he said, but finding his near relation, General Thaw, engaged the attention of every body, he had taken his leave for a short time.

I was going to pay the General a visit, when a desperate contest arose between Sir Partial and General Frost. It appeared that the latter had so long occupied the space under the stern, that he deemed Sir Partial's visit an infringement on his prerogative, and that Sir Partial, from dictates of humanity, was desirous of expelling him from his post, and ridding the ships of a very disagreeable and intruding visitor, who, he said was not contented with remaining on the upper-deck, but, on finding a difficulty in getting down the hatchways, had had the impudence to creep in at the cabin window. The General was obdurate, and Sir Partial finding knock-down arguments did not succeed, endeavoured by gentle means to soften the General into compliance, and was so successful, that he was content to sculk behind a cask for a considerable time, until Sir Partial was gone, when he stole out by degrees.   N.

To the EDITOR *of the* Winter Chronicle.

SIR—Having accidentally heard it rumoured, that it is in contemplation to send off a certain number of balloons, with letters containing an account of our situation, &c., it has occurred to me, that it would be a good opportunity of conveying also to England a copy of the *Winter Chronicle*, by which our friends might be informed before-hand, in what manner we have endeavoured to drive away the *ennui* of a winter in North Georgia. Indeed, I know no mode of conveyance so exactly suited to most of the productions which fill the pages of your Journal. There are many which being, as the writers confess, " the lightest things imaginable," are peculiarly fit for this kind of travelling: and, I think it is not impossible, that some of your correspondents, if requested, might furnish an article or two light enough to assist the balloons in their aërial voyage, so as to economize the inflammable gas, which, with the heavier productions, must, as you will readily allow, be used in profuse abundance. Even the heaviest of them, however might perhaps, with good management, and a little clipping and curtailing, be made to rise much above the level which has hitherto been assigned to them by your readers; but whether this is expecting too much of the inflammable air, I leave to your more scientific correspondents to determine.

Such communications as consist of high-flown language, lofty conceptions, elevated sentiments, &c., will find themselves quite at home when thus conveyed among the clouds: and our poets who kindly furnish their weekly quota of rhymes for our amusement, and who have hitherto had the mortification to see their works confined to earth, like mere vulgar prose, may now hope to behold the efforts of their respective muses, keep pace with the most poetical imagination, and soaring aloft into " Heaven's vast concave," take a higher flight than even Pegasus himself ever attempted. In pursuance of the plan which I have here proposed, it would be adding much to the obligation you have already conferred upon the public as Editor of the Gazette, if you would employ a few of your leisure moments, in selecting such articles from your columns as appear to you best qualified for the respective purposes of carrying or being carried; and it will naturally occur to you, that the fairest way of executing this useful project will be to tack a light and a heavy one in the same parcel, and thus to consign them to the atmosphere. For example, if the letter of Z, in your last Number but one, which was universally allowed to be a heavy one, and that of " N. C.", in a former one, were pinned into one bundle, there would, perhaps, be little left for the gas to do. And so of many others, which your ingenuity will easily enable you to couple in a similar manner.

I am, Sir,
Your most obedient,
HILARY HIGH-FLYER.

For the WINTER CHRONICLE.

Deus nos ducat *.

To lie in bed and meditate,
And then success anticipate,
Until my heart did palpitate,
    Has been my greatest pleasure.

When cold has set me shaking,
And sleep my eyes forsaking,
Our glorious undertaking
    Has warmed me beyond measure.

When pain has set me whining,
And health has been declining,
What kept me from repining ?
    'Twas Hope, and trust above!

God is our shield defensive
Throughout the world extensive,
His mercy comprehensive,
    Deserves our warmest love.

Should hardships overtake us,
Let them nor danger shake us,
Our God will ne'er forsake us,
    Who worketh all for good !

* The motto upon the binnacle of the Hecla.

When perils bid defiance
To human skill and science,
On *Him* be our reliance
　　Who shed for us his blood !

SONG FROM THE NORTH-WEST PASSAGE.

WRITTEN BY MR. WAKEHAM,

AND SUNG BY MR. PALMER.

I.

FAREWELL to the land where the winter we 've past,
The ships all a-taunt-to, we leave it at last,
　　While our bosoms are swelling
　　For deeds of renown ;
Beneath their snug housing the cold we've defied,
We 've tripp'd for our health o'er the firm frozen tide,
And merrily keeping up cheerfulness still,
Eat our grub, drank our grog, with a hearty good will,
　　While our bosoms were swelling
　　For deeds of renown.

II.

'Tis said, when the sun in this region sinks low,
The bears take a long nap—but we did not so,
　　While our bosoms were swelling
　　For deeds of renown ;
We had snow to be melted, ere dinner was drest,
We had beer to be brew'd, and 'twas some of the best :—
But what most I admired, while we wanted the light,
Were the plays that amused us once a fort-night,
　　While our bosoms were swelling
　　For deeds of renown,

III.

Before it was dark in this desolate spot,
The deer came around us, and died by our shot,
　　While our bosoms were swelling
　　For deeds of renown.
With venison and beef, we cared not the least
For the famed turtle soup of an alderman's feast ;

A sailor lives well, if he gets but enough
Of something substantial, or tender or tough,
    While our bosoms are swelling
    For deeds of renown.

IV.

Now the day-light's return'd, we'll push on without fear,
And prove to our country that while lying here,
    Still our bosoms were swelling
    For deeds of renown.
If ice should impede us, our progress tho' slow,
We'll advance all we can; if wind fails us we'll tow;
If channels are opened, our ships track'd along
Shall follow us close, and we'll tune up a song,
    While our bosoms are swelling
    For deeds of renown;

V.

The voyage completed, and doubled Cape Horn,
How joyful we'll hail the bright blush of the morn,
    While our bosoms are swelling
    For deeds of renown;
That shews us again that loved rock of our isle,
Where around us our wives and our little ones smile.
And rewards that await us return'd from afar,
Prove how warmly Old England remembers the tar,
    While our bosoms are swelling
    For deeds of renown.

SONG FROM THE NORTH-WEST PASSAGE.

WRITTEN BY MR. WAKEHAM,
AND SUNG BY MR. HOPPNER.

Tune—" *Come cheer up, my lads.*"

I.

At last brother tars here we are at the strait,
And the famed North-West Passage is travers'd complete;
O'er the wide rolling waves to the southward we'll steer,
And quickly arrive at the land of good cheer.
    In the ice of the north British hearts were our own,
        Still seeking for glory,
        Famous in story,
We've gain'd for Old England new ways of renown.

II.

'Mid darkness and storms a longer winter we stay'd,
While the crystallized ocean our efforts delay'd,
Till summer returning again set us free,
And open'd the way to that far western sea.
  In the ice of the north British hearts were our own,
      Still seeking for glory,
      Famous in story,
  We've gain'd for Old England new ways of renown.

III.

What feelings of pleasure, what joys shall expand,
When once more we're nearing, fair Albion, thy strand ;
Delighted our bosoms with transport shall swell,
And fondly each tongue of its happiness tell.
  In the ice of the north British hearts were our own,
      Still seeking for glory,
      Famous in story,
  We ve gain'd for Old England new ways of renown.

IV.

Our country shall hail our emprize with acclaim,
Attempted for ages by chieftains of fame ;
For firm perseverance evinced in her cause,
Has ever yet met with true Britons' applause.
  In the ice of the north British hearts were our own,
      Still seeking for glory,
      Famous in story,
  We've gain'd for Old England new ways of renown.

THE
NORTH GEORGIA GAZETTE,

AND
WINTER CHRONICLE.

N°. XXI—MONDAY, MARCH 20, 1820.

To the EDITOR *of the* Winter Chronicle.

SIR,

I HEAR it said that the North Georgia Gazette is soon to die a natural death, and I am sorry for it ; for then must your correspondent Z. leave half his purpose unfinished.—" Othello's occupation's gone ! "

I had prepared a letter in pursuance of my former plan ; but as I am informed that this is the last communication which I shall have an opportunity of laying before your readers, during this season, I suppose I must change my note, and be upon my good behaviour.

It has been very amusing, and I must add very flattering to me, to hear the conjectures which have been formed concerning the author of Z.'s letters, and the remarks which have been made upon them by the individuals of our community ; and I am not altogether without hope that I have done something towards removing, at least in part, the annoyances of which I complained.

A friend of mine in London, who has a share in a patent-shot manufactory, once explained to me the manner in which the round or perfect shot are separated from those which are oval, and therefore unfit for use. Being all made to roll down an inclined plane, the round ones roll straight forward to the lower end, while the oval ones are found to waddle to the edge of the plane, and fall over before they can reach the bottom. I have often been reminded of this contrivance, in observing that the *Whistlers, Slammers, &c. &c. &c.,* have waddled on one side when applied to the inclined plane afforded by Z.'s communications, and have immediately fallen into the ranks, under the several heads to which, according to their respective qualifications, they know themselves to belong. Some of them have not much relished being made to waddle in this manner, and would rather have been allowed to roll on straight forward to the end of the chapter. This is all very natural, but it is no fault of mine; they are no shot of my making. I think I have done them some service in pointing out their deformity; and if they will get their oval ends rounded off before the recommencement of the News-papers, I promise them they shall hear no more from Z.

But, to be serious, if the annoyances to which my letters allude are real, they ought to be remedied ;—if imaginary, if nobody practises them, then is there no " galled jade to wince,"—all our " withers are unwrung,"—in short, if the cap fits nobody, let nobody wear it !

But since the game is up for the present, I have no hesitation in assuring you and your readers, that the classes described in my first letter are as completely the creatures of imagination, as ever entered into the head of a poet. I had at that time no intention of continuing my correspondence, much less had I conceived any thing like a regular series of such descriptions. It was your readers themselves who first put this into my head, and made me look about me for such subjects, as well by the hints with which their remarks daily furnished me, as by the earnest applications made to me, through the medium of your paper. It was then, and then only, that I began to be really in earnest, and to copy from life. For instance, the public are wholly indebted for the description I have endeavoured to give of the *Snorers*, to the unnconscious suggestions of one of that dozing fraternity; and the same is true of the more innocent *Stampers*. As for the *Slammers*, it is more than probable that they would have

remained altogether unknown to Z., unless they had been pointed out to his notice by his correspondent X.; and so of one or two other classes.

So much for the account I purposed to give of my letters ; may I be permitted to say a word or two of myself, as it is a subject which has afforded me much entertainment. There is scarcely one among us who has not hazarded a conjecture who Z is. One I find " knows me well;" a second has found me out by the shortness of my sentences ; another " detects me at first sight," by a certain fault in my grammar, of which he has observed I am often guilty in conversation ; a fourth declares it " impossible to mistake me," though he does not say why, " and wonders at the want of discernment in those who are at a loss about me;" and a fifth is " quite positive" who I am, on account of a particular turn of expression which always was, is still, and ever will be mine, and mine exclusively.

A messmate took me aside the other day, and with a look full of mysterious importance, told me in confidence that he knew who Z. was. " Do you really?" said I; " Yes, it is so and so." " No! is it indeed?" " Yes," replied my cunning messmate, with a knowing shake of the head, " I had it from good authority." Thinks I to myself, you know nothing at all about it; but I promised to keep his secret, and so I will.

The truth is, Mr. Editor, that having for the first ten weeks of the publication of your paper openly avowed my incapacity or unwillingness to write for it, and, to my shame be it recorded, even spoke disrespectfully of a scheme of amusement to which I was myself too indolent to contribute, I have found myself securely sheltered of late under my former declaration, and have thus been induced to join in the general laugh, or to put up with any occasional expression of displeasure with as much apparent unconcern as any I see about me. It is no great wonder that others do not easily find *him* out, who has hardly been able to persuade *himself* that he has written.

When children play at hide and seek, they are told that they " burn" when they come near the hiding-place; but I can assure those who have searched for Z., that they have never been warm, no not within a mile of the fire; they are all equally knowing, and all equally wrong.

Adieu, Mr. Editor, for the present. I trust my next communication may be the growth of a more genial climate; may it spring up amidst the rich luxuriance of the South Sea Islands! Believe me, there are none of your correspondents or readers who entertain this hope more confidently, and who are willing to do more towards its completion, than your

Unknown and obedient Servant,
Z.

————

SIR,—As I was one of the first among your correspondents to address you at the commencement of your editorial labours, and to express my good wishes for the success of your undertaking, so I am equally desirous, now that I understand your paper is shortly to be discontinued, to express to you the gratification I have derived from the spirit with which the Winter Chronicle has been supported for one-and-twenty weeks, and the amusement I have received from many of its pages, during that tedious interval.

As an individual of that community to whose amusement you have, during the winter, devoted a certain weekly portion of your time, I am anxious to convey to you my share of the acknowledgment which is so justly your due. Nor can I omit to express my obligation to the two gentlemen whose zeal in the cause of good humour and cheerfulness has in-duced them to copy, with unceasing punctuality, for our perusal, the various communications with which your box has been furnished. It will be generally allowed that the original purpose of the Winter Chronicle has been completely answered. It has certainly served to " exercise the ingenuity" of several of our community; and we have seen it raise many a laugh, and many a hearty one too, at a time when in the ordinary course of our affairs, there was little or nothing to make us smile ; and besides the amusement it has afforded at the time of reading it, I have observed that some of the articles in each paper, have usually furnished subject for good-humoured conversation during the ensuing week, at the expiration of which a fresh supply has been brought forward to fulfil the same end. It will, perhaps, be objected by some of your more serious readers, that the time thus spent might have been better employed; to which I may reply, that it might also have been worse employed, or even not employed *at all.* " Better do mischief than do nothing," says the proverb, and the spirit, if not the letter of this maxim, is right.

But it is said that there are one or two of your readers who have not derived so much amusement from the perusal of your papers, as the rest of us, and who are even said to be rather offended at some of the waggish communications contained in them. If this be the case, which, however, I can scarcely believe, there is now no remedy for it : but I will venture to assert, that no one article has been penned with any intention of giving offence to an individual of our party.

We are now, Mr. Editor, to enter on a different occupation, in which all your readers, whether contributors or non-contributors, will, I am sure most cordially join; and I hope yet to see those at whose expense a laugh has occasionally been raised in the Winter Chronicle, laugh in their turn when they shall see their names occupying a more honourable place in the London Gazette.

I am, Mr. Editor,

Your obliged and obedient Servant,

PHILO-COMUS.

To the EDITOR of the Winter Chronicle.

Mr. EDITOR,

Before your papers cease for this season, allow me to insert some wishes which I most fervently entertain, and in which I doubt not that many of your readers will join with me.

First, then, I wish your entertaining papers may appear at our breakfast-table with the very first Monday after our housing is put over the ships the next winter—should such again be the case.

Next, I wish an early summer to such as want to go westward, and eternal frost to those whose minds are bent the other way—if any such there be.

I wish a safe passage to the rein-deer, a southerly wind to the ducks, and success to the sportsmen.

I wish an idle birth to our doctors for the remainder of the voyage, and a day's sickness to those who lightly treat the complaints of others.

I wish a speedy sight of Behring's Straits to the sanguine, disappointment to the desponders, and moderation to boasters.

To advocates for cold, I wish frost-bitten fingers; and to complainers of it, a vertical sun.

I wish to husbands patience, to their wives constancy, and to lovers fidelity.

Lastly, I wish perfect health to every one; the pleasure of revisiting our native country to all; reformation to Snorers, Slammers, Bangers, &c.; success to our voyage, and pleasure to my readers.

I am, Mr. Editor,

Your well-wisher,

T.

THEATRICAL REPORT.

On Thursday evening was performed the farce of the *Citizen*; to which was added the *Mayor of Garratt*; being the last of our Theatrical Entertainments for the season. At the end of the last scene an appropriate and animated *Farewell Address*, from the pen of Mr. Wakeham, was spoken by that gentleman in the character of a Sailor, and received with the most rapturous applause. The whole concluded with *God save the King*, in which all the performers, as well as most of the audience joined; and the curtain fell amidst the loud and hearty cheers of the whole house. Our readers will find a copy of the Address, with which we have been favoured, in the subsequent pages of this Number.

Thus has ended a series of Dramatic Entertainments, which have served to beguile the tedious season of a long and cheerless winter. In the progress of these entertainments, we have taken frequent occasion to express our conviction of the good effect which this kind of amusement has produced among those for whose diversion they were chiefly, if not exclusively, intended; and we may now add, that each successive representation has tended to confirm the conviction.

The promotion of cheerfulness among the men was an object which, in our present situation, called for our best exertions. To persons possessing no sources of amusement within themselves, some such means were more than usually necessary, especially in a climate where the rugged aspect of nature has little to enliven the mind, or to dissipate the gloom of despondency.

The good consequences resulting from the unremitted exertions that have been made to attain this desirable end, cannot, perhaps, be sufficiently apprehended at present; their influence may be expected to extend to the latest period of our voyage, and may, perhaps, be hereafter considered as having materially, though indirectly, contributed to the ultimate success of our enterprise.

THEATRE ROYAL, NORTH GEORGIA.

The Manager and Committee take this public method of returning their best thanks to the gentlemen who have so liberally contributed towards the support of the theatre.

Nor can they let the opportunity pass without expressing the high gratification they have received in the discharge of their duty as Committee-men, from the willingness with which each gentleman has endeavoured to support the characters which have been assigned to him, and from the good-humour and unanimity which have prevailed throughout the season.

For the last Number of the **WINTER CHRONICLE.**

COME Muse, and attend to my last invocation,
    Come mourn with your pupil the Chronicle's close!
No more shall we hear Monday morn's titteration,
    That welcomed its pages in verse or in prose.

What wonders perform'd by its two sheets per week!
    How strain'd our invention and faculties all!
If half the bulkheads of the cabins could speak,
    They'd shew that invention, nor feeble, nor small.

Fair Dames it has brought to North Georgia's shore,
    Manufactured a ghost and an animal strange;
That (named the *Encea*) you 'll hear of no more
    In forests or floods through all nature's wide range.

Here you and your sisters inspired our gay youth,
    Till " Heaven's vast concave" resounded their songs ;—
Much nonsense we 've read, and a great deal of truth,
    Well-founded complaints, and some fanciful wrongs.

Ev'n loggerheads well could contribute their shares
    To the weekly contents of the Editor's box ;
The world was soon told of our weighty affairs,
    The death of a gull, or escape of a fox.

There's Q in the corner, with X, Y, and P,
    Philo-Comus and Albert, and Simon Set-right,
Maria and Emily, fair maids I see,
    And Anti-scalp Anne, not in charms quite so bright.

There 's a posse besides, but by naming them all
    I patience and paper should equally waste ;
The meanings of some would a counsellor pall :—
    But now to lament their misfortunes I haste.

The Plays and the Papers together expire,
    And Poets, and Actors, and Dames breathe their last ;
To soothe parting moments I 'll say that their fire
    Has not, in this region, been ever surpass'd.

Wintry wits of the North ! who have scribbled away
    To shave or amuse us, accept a sad sigh
From one who has sometimes attempted a lay ;
    And thus, Brother-Scribblers, I bid you good-bye!

A FAREWELL ADDRESS

WRITTEN AND SPOKEN BY MR. WAKEHAM IN THE CHARACTER OF A SAILOR, AT THE FINAL CLOSE OF THE PERFORMANCES AT THE NORTH GEORGIA THEATRE.

DREAR was the night that Nature's face o'erspread,
When light's last gleam this sadden'd region fled ;
No active scenes disarm'd its torpid power,
Nor soft society beguiled the hour ;
The dark dull season call'd for other aid,
Our comic talents then we each essay'd—
Here Garrick's heroes mimick passions move,
And list'ning ladies melt at tales of love ;
For woman's semblance graced our Georgian stage,
The strangest medley of the present age ;—
A paper bonnet oft her head embraced,
Her canvass stays were by a sailor laced,
The dress in which her beauty sought to shine
Form'd and arranged by fingers masculine !—
Her ribbons, painted—tin, her glitt'ring fan—
Bright beads her diamonds, and herself—a man !
The Drama's beaux were not to be outdone,—
Fox-hunting squires in paper boot-tops shone,—
And the plump landlord, when he took a swig,
Conceal'd his blushes by an Oakum wig,—

Tin spurs, and paper frills for Dandies made,
And bear-skin whiskers help'd the gay parade :—
But jesting o'er—to-night the plays we close,
For passing winter asks no more repose.

As the brave soldier, on the martial field
O'erborne by tenfold odds and forced to yield,
Press'd by the captive chain feels not its weight,
When on the thunders of the nearer fight
His fate suspended hangs, till Vict'ry's tide
Proclaims the conquer'd now the conqu'ring side ;
Then freed once more he shines in radiant arms,
And mingling eager in the war's alarms
Feels the new wrong within his bosom glow,
And bursts indignant on th' embattled foe.
So we, secured by Winter's icy chain,
Awhile the pris'ners of its gloomy reign,
Hear in the blast that sweeps the frozen sea
The friendly sound that soon shall set us free,
When hasting forward with impatient force
Hope's cheering ray shall gild our Western course.

If from the past our future scenes we trace,
The prospect wears an animating face,
For providential mercies open wide,
And show that fav'ring Heaven has been our guide.
When in our front the ice opposing lay,
Still thro' the mass we found a devious way,—
If humid fogs obscured the mid-day sun
From ev'ry danger safe, we still have run :—
Unfaithful here the guiding needle flies,
Now points to Northern, now to Southern skies ;
But ever have we kept the path design'd,
And left the distant Eastern shores behind.
What breast unconscious of the heav'nly Hand
That saved our vessels from the fatal strand,
When far extended floes with headlong sway
Drove fiercely shoreward in yon western bay ?—
Yet morning's light, tho' human help was vain,
Beheld us riding on the liquid main :
And still, I trust, that Hand, which rules o'er all,
Which guides the motions of this whirling ball,
Will lead us onward thro the icy road
To where the southern joins the polar flood,
Until at length that happy morn appears
When Behring's Strait shall echo British cheers.

Sons of my country ! in her cause allied,
A sailor's feelings are my bosom's pride,—
Those feelings tell me that each brother tar
Exults in cherish'd hope,—advanced thus far—
The hope that soon success shall crown our toil,
And honours greet us on our native soil.
Britannia's hopes are centred in our deeds—
To this emprize the path of glory leads !—
Her ancient chiefs of ever-honour'd name,
Call on us now to emulate their fame :—
Each tender tie that deep infixes *here*,
Bids us our country and ourselves revere :
Then, sailors, thus I 'll your resolve express,
" We *can't command*, but *will deserve* success."

THE Editor would be ill satisfied with himself were he to permit the *Winter Chronicle* to conclude without expressing his thanks to his Correspondents *generally*, for the courtesy with which they have addressed him ; and to those gentlemen *particularly*, who have principally supported the Paper, for the readiness with which they have at all times attended to his request of contributions, and frequently at a very short notice.

His more than thanks are due and are felt to his two friends who have so cheerfully and kindly taken on themselves, even from the commencement, the manual duties of the editorial office ; leaving to the Editor himself little more than the honour of the name.

Winter Harbour, March 18, 1820.

THE END

LONDON:
PRINTED BY WILLIAM CLOWES,
Northumberland-court.

www.ingramcontent.com/pod-product-compliance
Ingram Content Group UK Ltd.
Pitfield, Milton Keynes, MK11 3LW, UK
UKHW012022280225
455719UK00011B/439